Baal

Works of Bertolt Brecht published by Arcade

Baal

The Caucasian Chalk Circle

Collected Stories

The Good Person of Setzuan, adapted by Tony Kushner

The Good Person of Szechwan

The Good Person of Szechwan, Mother Courage and Her Children, and *Fear and Misery of the Third Reich*

Life of Galileo

Life of Galileo, The Resistible Rise of Arturo Ui, and *The Caucasian Chalk Circle*

Mother Courage and Her Children

Mother Courage and Her Children, adapted by David Hare

Mr. Puntila and His Man Matti

The Rise and Fall of the City of Mahagonny and *The Seven Deadly Sins of the Petty Bourgeoisie*

Saint Joan of the Stockyards

The Threepenny Opera

The Threepenny Opera, Baal, and *The Mother*

BERTOLT BRECHT

Baal

Translated from the German by Peter Tegel

Edited by John Willett and Ralph Manheim

ARCADE PUBLISHING • NEW YORK

FIRST ARCADE PAPERBACK EDITION 1998

Baal, originally published in German under the title *Baal*, was first published in this translation in 1970.

ISBN 1-55970-419-5
Library of Congress Catalog Card Number 98-72438
Library of Congress Cataloging-in-Publication information is available.

Published in the United States by Arcade Publishing, Inc., New York
Distributed by Little, Brown and Company

10 9 8 7 6 5 4 3 2 1

CCP

PRINTED IN THE UNITED STATES OF AMERICA

Introduction

1

Baal is the first of four full-length plays (the others being *Drums in the Night, In the Jungle of Cities* and *The Life of Edward II of England*) which Brecht wrote in Bavaria before moving to Berlin in the autumn of 1924. In spring 1918, when he began work on the first of them, he was just twenty and a new student at Munich university. Six and a half years later he was a recognized, if controversial writer and the winner of a major literary prize. The best directors and actors of the day were performing his plays; he had also written many poems and short stories and directed one remarkable production. He had just been on the staff of the Munich Kammerspiele, one of the most enterprising small theatres in Germany, where his first and so far most successful play had been performed. Now he was about to go as a 'dramaturg', or literary adviser, to Max Reinhardt's Deutsches Theater in Berlin, at that time one of the world's three or four leading theatres.

Born on 10 February 1898, Brecht had been brought up in Augsburg, about forty miles west of Munich. His father, a native of the Black Forest, was sales director of the Haindl paper works there; his mother died in May 1920. *Baal*, whose first version was finished by July 1918, reflects much of the imaginary world of himself and his group of Augsburg friends, as well as the taverns and physical surroundings of the old city. For a few months just before and after the armistice of November 1918 he served as a medical orderly in a local army hospital, but had returned to Munich by February 1919, the early days of the Bavarian Soviet, during which he dashed off the first version of *Drums in the Night*. There he showed both plays to Lion Feuchtwanger, the author of *Jew Süss*, who was then living in Munich and had recently met him for the first time. His own drama professor Artur Kutscher was always bitterly critical of his work, but Feuchtwanger was encouraging, so that he began to make contact with publishers and, at the end of the summer vacation, to write theatre criticisms for the Augsburg Socialist paper. Five one-act plays, *A Respectable Wedding, The Beggar, Driving out a Devil, Lux in Tenebris* and *The Catch*, are also thought to have been mainly written that year, as well as a wealth of lost or unfinished works.

Baal was accepted by Feuchtwanger's own publisher Georg Müller, who had also published Wedekind's collected plays, but was withdrawn when already in proof for fear of the censorship. *Drums in the Night* was shown by Feuchtwanger to the Kammerspiele 'dramaturg' Rudolf Frank, who at some point in the summer of 1920 accepted it for production. Neither publication nor production in fact materialized for another two years, but the encouragement to Brecht was obvious. He left the university in the summer of 1921 and in November set out to try his luck in Berlin, a much more important city from the theatrical point of view.

The expedition was less successful than he had hoped. Neither the Deutsches Theater nor the State Theatre under Leopold Jessner would make any promises, and although Brecht was asked to direct Arnolt Bronnen's play *Vatermord* for the experimental Junge Bühne, it ended disastrously with a walk-out of the actors. He himself was taken to hospital suffering from undernourishment, due no doubt in part to the galloping currency inflation. But at least he made many connections or friendships which were to be important for his work: notably Bronnen (with whom he began collaborating on film treatments and various joint theatrical projects), Herbert Ihering the critic of the *Berliner Börsen-Courier* (a lifelong supporter, whose paper was later to serve as a launching-platform for many of his ideas), and Moritz Seeler the organizer of the Junge Bühne (who was to produce *Life Story of the Man Baal* in 1926). By the time of his return to Augsburg at Easter he had also completed the first version of *In the Jungle*.

In Bavaria 1922 was a Brecht year. Soon after his return the Munich Residenztheater accepted *In the Jungle*, and *Baal* was at last published (by Gustav Kiepenheuer of Potsdam), while 29 September saw the première of *Drums in the Night*. Ihering came from Berlin to review it, and in the *Berliner Börsen-Courier* of 5 October he wrote that 'At 24 the writer Bert Brecht has changed Germany's literary complexion overnight. Bert Brecht has given our time a new tone, a new melody, a new vision.' Here too was 'a physical sense of chaos and decay':

> Hence the unparallelled creative force of his language. It is a language you can feel on your tongue, in your gums, your ear, your spinal column.

Ihering was known to be the judge for that year's award of the Kleist Prize. This had been founded in 1911 by a group of Kleist enthusiasts to celebrate the centenary of the poet's death, and was intended for writers who had yet to establish themselves. Up to its abolition in 1932 it was probably the most significant literary award in Germany, having previously been given to the playwrights Sorge, Unruh, Hasenclever and Jahnn, while in 1923–5 it went to Musil, Barlach and Zuckmayer. On 13 November the *Berliner Börsen-Courier* announced that it had gone to Brecht, and not for *Drums in the Night* only but for all three of his completed plays. 'Brecht's linguistic power,' said Ihering's citation,

> is even more richly developed in *Baal* and *In the Jungle*. His language is vivid without being deliberately poetic, symbolical without being over literary. Brecht is a dramatist because his language is felt physically and in the round.

That October Brecht was appointed to the Kammerspiele's dramaturgical and directing staff, where his main task was the adaptation and production of Marlowe's *Edward II*. The actual writing of this play, which is very largely an original work, must have taken place mainly in the winter of 1922–3, since the Berlin State Theatre started showing an interest in it early in the new year.

It was done in collaboration with Feuchtwanger, whom Brecht saw frequently throughout 1923. It was not however performed till the next year, and although there were two more Brecht premières in 1923, neither was at the Kammerspiele itself. First *In the Jungle* was staged at the Residenztheater on 9 May by Erich Engel, with settings by Brecht's school-friend Caspar Neher: the beginning of a lifelong collaboration between the three men. But the three-hour performance was poorly received; it ran for only six evenings, and altogether was a disastrous enough flop to occasion the sacking of the theatre's artistic adviser. Nor was *Baal* in Leipzig at the end of the year any more successful. Alvin Kronacher's production at the Old Theatre on 8 December was taken off by order of the city council within a week, and the director reprimanded. It brought an interesting press controversy between Ihering and his rival Alfred Kerr as to the relative originality of Brecht and Toller, but Kerr was undoubtedly right when he wrote that 'The only hope for a Baalade like this is as a posthumous fragment . . .'. For the text as we have it was not performed again for another forty years.

II

If the Bavarian years made Brecht's name they also established the main lines of argument for and against his work, with Kerr and Ihering respectively as counsel for the prosecution and the defence. Already the point at issue was his literary borrowings, and a number of later attacks on him were foreshadowed in Kerr's *Baal* critique, with its dismissal of the play as second-hand Büchner and Grabbe. 'The gifted Brecht,' he wrote, 'is a frothing plagiarist.' To which Ihering countered:

> A writer's productivity can be seen in his relationship with old themes. In *Schweiger* Werfel invented a 'hitherto unheard of story' and was none the less imitative in every respect. Brecht was fired by Marlowe's *Edward II* and was creative through and through.

At the same time Brecht had been able to build the nucleus of his subsequent team of supporters and collaborators: first and foremost Neher, then Engel, the rather older Feuchtwanger, Fritz Kortner, Oskar Homolka, Klabund's actress wife Carola Neher and the playwright Marieluise Fleisser, all of them people who have left their individual marks on the German theatre. Here Brecht's personal magnetism clearly played a part: something to which there have been many tributes, starting with Feuchtwanger's fictional picture of him as the engineer Pröckl in his novel *Success* (1931).

These were Brecht's pre-collectivist, indeed in a sense his pre-political years. He undoubtedly had opinions, many of them progressive and even revolutionary, but they were far from systematic, and politics and economics were wholly absent from what we know of his reading. On the other hand it was an extraordinarily tense and eventful time for Germany in general and Bavaria in particular, and Brecht was much too sensitive a writer not to reflect this in his work. A good deal has been made of his supposed pacifism in the First World War — though his schoolboy writings show that in fact he set out from a conventionally patriotic attitude and hardly developed beyond concern at the casualties — and of the impact made on him by his military service, which in fact was done on his own doorstep and in a hospital for venereal diseases, and started only a month or two before the end of the war. Several of the *Hauspostille* poems which are held to express his post-war sense of release had in fact already been written by then. Nor is there any evidence that he was more than a spectator of the revolutionary movements of November 1918, when the monarchy fell, and the first months of 1919, when Munich and Augsburg were governed by Soviets following Kurt Eisner's murder and the short-lived Spartacist revolt in Berlin.

The element of revolt in his writing of this time was largely directed against his own middle-class background: the satirical first scene of *Baal*, for instance, and the first two acts of *Drums in the Night*. Much of his reading, too, was exotic-escapist, as can be seen from the allusions in these early plays to Gauguin and *Treasure Island* and Rudyard Kipling, and certainly this partly explains Brecht's interest in Rimbaud, whose elevated prose underlies Gargar's 'psalmodizing' in *In the Jungle* (cf. Brecht's own semi-prose 'Psalms') and whose relationship with Verlaine was surely the model for that of Baal and Ekart.

The years 1918–1924 saw not only a certain element of political restoration throughout central and eastern Europe but also the end of Expressionism in the arts. To the poet-playwright Iwan Goll, who in 1921 published an essay called 'Expressionism is Dying', the two phenomena were connected. 'Expressionism was a fine, good, grand thing . . .' he wrote. 'But the result is, alas, and through no fault of the Expressionists, the German Republic of 1920.' Dadaism likewise was breaking up by 1922; at the Bauhaus the semi-mystical Itten was about to be succeeded by the technologically minded Moholy-Nagy; while artists like Grosz, Dix, Beckmann and Schlichter were evolving the coolly representational, socially conscious style which in 1924 became known as *Neue Sachlichkeit*. Brecht was always much too conscious of his own aims to care to be labelled as part of a movement; none the less his works of these years very clearly reflect the decline of Expressionism and the rise of the new style. He defined his position admirably in a note of 27 June 1920:

> I can compete with the ultra-modernists in hunting for new forms and experimenting with my feelings. But I keep realizing that the essence of art is simplicity, grandeur and sensitivity, and that the essence of its form is coolness.

Baal was written as a kind of counter-play to the Expressionists' invocations of Humanity with a capital H, yet the wandering poet remains a romantic-expressionist figure, while the influence of Georg Büchner is one that is also noticeable in a number of Expressionist plays. *Drums in the Night* too, with its symbolic use of the moon, its cinematic third act and its hero's slightly mad rhetoric, can reasonably be termed an Expressionist play. *In the Jungle*, however, was written at the turning-point, the watershed between the two movements. The Rimbaud allusions, the colour references before each scene in the 1922 version, the attic-cum-undergrowth setting, the use of spotlights referred to in Brecht's note of 1954: all this is expressionistic, whereas the American milieu, the pre-occupation with the big cities and the very notion of the 'fight' were to become characteristic concerns of the mid-1920s. A further note of 10 February 1922 even suggests that Brecht was looking forward to his own 1930s doctrine of 'alienation':

> I hope in *Baal* and *Jungle* I've avoided one common artistic bloomer, that of trying to carry people away. Instinctively, I've kept my distance and ensured that the realization of my (poetical and philosophical) effects remains within bounds. The spectator's 'splendid isolation' is left intact; it is not *sua res quae agitur*; he is not fobbed off with an invitation to feel sympathetically, to fuse with the hero and seem significant and indestructible as he watches himself in two different versions. A higher type of interest can be got from making comparisons, from whatever is different, amazing, impossible to overlook.

Thus though *In the Jungle* is still wildly romantic it already foreshadows the detached impersonalities of the machine age. And those supporters who, like Ihering and Engel and Geis, thought that Brecht would help lead the theatre out of the Expressionist undergrowth can now be seen to have been absolutely right.

THE EDITORS

Note: A full version of this Introduction appears in the hardback edition of Brecht's *Collected Plays, Volume 1 1918–1923*.

Baal

To my friend George Pfanzelt

Translator: PETER TEGEL

Characters

Baal, poet · Mech, merchant and publisher · Emilie, his wife · Dr Piller, critic · Johannes Schmidt · Pschierer, director of the water rates · a young man · a young woman · Johanna · Ekart · Luise, a waitress · the two sisters · the landlady · Sophie Barger · the tramp · Lupu · Mjurk · the nightclub singer · a pianist · the parson · Bolleboll · Gougou · the old beggar · Maja, the beggarwoman · the young woman · Watzmann · a waitress · two policemen · drivers · peasants · woodcutters

HYMN OF BAAL THE GREAT

Baal grew up within the whiteness of the womb
With the sky already large and pale and calm
Naked, young, endlessly marvellous
As Baal loved it when he came to us.

And that sky remained with him through joy and care
Even when Baal slept, blissful and unaware.
Nights meant violet sky and drunken Baal
Dawns, Baal good, sky apricottish-pale.

So through hospital, cathedral, bar
Baal trots coolly on, and learns to let them go.
When Baal's tired, boys, Baal will not fall far:
Baal will drag his whole sky down below.

Where the sinners herd in shame together
Baal lies naked, soaking up the calm.
Just the sky, but sky to last for *ever*
Hides his nakedness with its strong arm.

And that lusty girl, the world, who laughs when yielding
To the man who'll stand the pressure of her thighs
Gives him instants of a sweet ecstatic feeling.
Baal survives it; he just looks and sees.

And when Baal sees corpses all around
Then a double pleasure comes to him.
Lots of space, says Baal; they're not enough to count.
Lots of space inside this woman's womb.

Once a woman, Baal says, gives her all
She'll have nothing more, so let her go!
Other men would represent no risk at all.
Even Baal is scared of babies, though.

Vice, says Baal, is bound to help a bit
And so are the men who practise it.
Vices leave their mark on all they touch.
Stick to two, for one will be too much.

Slackness, softness – that's what you should shun.
Nothing's tougher than pursuing fun.
Powerful limbs are needed, and experience too
Swollen bellies may discourage you.

Baal watches the vultures in the star-shot sky
Hovering patiently to see when Baal will die.
Sometimes Baal shams dead. The vultures swoop.
Baal, without a word, will dine on vulture soup.

Under mournful stars in our sad vale of trouble
Munching, Baal can graze broad pastures down to stubble.
When they're cropped, into the forest deep
Baal trots, singing, to enjoy his sleep.

And when Baal's dragged down to be the dark womb's prize
What's the world to Baal? Baal has been fed.
Sky enough still lurks behind Baal's eyes
To make just enough sky when he's dead.

Baal decayed within the darkness of the womb
With the sky once more as large and pale and calm
Naked, young, endlessly marvellous
As Baal loved it when he came to us.

Dining Room

Mech, Emilie Mech, Pschierer, Johannes Schmidt, Dr Piller, Baal and other guests enter through the revolving door.

MECH *to Baal:* Would you like some wine, Mr Baal? *All take seats, Baal in the place of honour.* Do you like crab? That's a dead eel.

PILLER *to Mech:* I'm very glad that the immortal poems of Mr Baal, which I had the honour of reading to you, have earned your approval. *To Baal:* You must publish your poetry. Mr Mech pays like a real patron of the arts. You'll be able to leave your attic.

MECH: I buy cinnamon wood. Whole forests of cinnamon float down the rivers of Brazil for my benefit. But I'll also publish your poetry.

EMILIE: You live in an attic?

BAAL *eating and drinking:* 64 Klauckestrasse.

MECH: I'm really too fat for poetry. But you've got the same-shaped head as a man in the Malayan Archipelago, who used to have himself driven to work with a whip. If he wasn't grinding his teeth he couldn't work.

PSCHIERER: Ladies and gentlemen. I admit it frankly: I was shattered to find a man like him in such modest circumstances. As you know, I discovered our dear poet in my office, a simple clerk. I have no hesitation in calling it a disgrace to our city that personalities of his calibre should be allowed to work for a daily wage. May I congratulate you, Mr Mech! Your salon will be famous as the cradle of this genius's, yes genius's, worldwide reputation. Your health, Mr Baal!

Baal wards off the speech with a gesture; he eats.

PILLER: I shall write an essay about you. Have you any manuscripts? I have the backing of the press.

A YOUNG MAN: How, my friend, do you get that accursed naïve effect? It's positively homeric. I consider Homer one, or rather one of several, highly civilized adapters with a penetrating delight in the naïveté of the original folk sagas.

A YOUNG LADY: You remind me more of Walt Whitman. But you're more significant. That's what I think.

ANOTHER MAN: I'd say he had something rather more of Verhaeren.

PILLER: Verlaine! Verlaine! Even in physiognomy. Don't forget our Lombroso.

BAAL: Some more of the eel, please.

THE YOUNG LADY: But you have the advantage of greater indecency.

JOHANNES: Mr Baal sings his songs to the lorry-drivers. In a café down by the river.

THE YOUNG MAN: Good God, none of those poets are even in the same category. My friend, you're streets ahead of any living poet.

THE OTHER MAN: At any rate he's promising.

BAAL: Some more wine please.

THE YOUNG MAN: I consider you a precursor of the great Messiah of European literature whom we can undoubtedly expect within the very near future.

THE YOUNG LADY: Dear poet, ladies, and gentlemen. Permit me to read you a poem from the periodical 'Revolution' which will also be of interest to you. *She rises and reads:*

The poet shuns shining harmonies.
He blows trombones, shrilly whips the drum.
He incites the people with chopped sentences.

The new world
Exterminating the world of pain,
Island of rapturous humanity.
Speeches. Manifestos.
Songs from grandstands.
Let there be preached the new,
The holy state, inoculated into the blood of the people,
Blood of their blood.

Paradise sets in.
– Let us spread a stormy climate!
Learn! Prepare! Practise!

Applause.

THE YOUNG LADY *quickly:* Permit me! I shall turn to another poem in the same issue. *She reads:*

Sun had made him shrivel
And wind had blown him dry.
By every tree rejected
He simply fell away.

Only a single rowan
With berries on every limb,
Red as flaming tongues, would
Receive and shelter him.

So there he hung suspended,
His feet lay on the grass.
The blood-red sunset splashed him
As through his ribs it passed.

It moved across the landscape
And struck all the olive groves.
God in his cloud-white raiment
Was manifest above.

Within the flowering forest
There sang a thousand snakes
While necks of purest silver
With slender murmurs shook.

And they were seized with trembling
All over that leafy domain
Obeying the hands of their Father
So light in their delicate veins.

Applause.

CRIES OF: Brilliant! Extreme but in good taste. Simply heavenly.

THE YOUNG LADY: In my opinion it comes closest to the Baalian conception of the world.

MECH: You should travel! The Abyssinian mountains. That's something for you.

BAAL: They won't come to me, though.

PILLER: Why? With your zest for life! Your poems had an enormous effect on me.

BAAL: The lorry-drivers pay if they like them.

MECH *drinking:* I'll publish your poems. I'll let the cinnamon logs float away, or do both.

EMILIE *to Mech:* You shouldn't drink so much.

BAAL: I haven't got any shirts. I could use some white shirts.

MECH: You're not interested in the publishing deal?

BAAL: But they'd have to be soft.

PILLER *ironic:* Oh, and what can I do for you?

EMILIE: You write such wonderful poems, Mr Baal. So sensitive.

BAAL *to Emilie:* Won't you play something on the harmonium?

Emilie plays.

MECH: I like eating to the harmonium.

EMILIE *to Baal:* Please don't drink so much, Mr Baal.

BAAL *looks at Emilie:* Do you have forests of cinnamon floating for you, Mech? Butchered forests?

EMILIE: You can drink as much as you like. I was only asking a favour.

PILLER: Even your drinking shows promise.

BAAL *to Emilie:* Play higher up! You've got lovely arms.

Emilie stops playing and approaches the table.

PILLER: Apparently you don't care for the music itself.

BAAL: I can't hear the music. You're talking too much.

PILLER: You're a queer fish, Baal. I gather you don't want to get published.

BAAL: Don't you trade in animals too, Mech?

MECH: Do you object?
BAAL *stroking Emilie's arm:* What's my poetry to you?
MECH: I wanted to do you a favour. Couldn't you be peeling some more apples, Emilie?
PILLER: He's afraid of being sucked dry. – Haven't you found a use for me yet?
BAAL: Do you always wear wide sleeves, Emilie?
PILLER: But now you really must stop drinking.
PSCHIERER: Perhaps you ought to go easy on the alcohol. Full many a genius —
MECH: Would you like to have a bath? Shall I have a bed made up for you? Have you forgotten anything?
PILLER: Your shirts are floating away, Baal. Your poetry has floated off already.
BAAL *drinks:* I'm against monopolies. Go to bed, Mech.
MECH *has risen:* I delight in all the animals on God's earth, but this is one animal you can't do business with. Come, Emilie! Shall we go, ladies and gentlemen?
All have risen indignantly.
CRIES: Sir! Astounding! That's the . . .!
PSCHIERER: I am shattered, Mr Mech . . .
PILLER: Your poetry has a malicious streak.
BAAL *to Johannes:* What is the gentleman's name?
JOHANNES: Piller.
BAAL: Well, Piller, *you* can send me some old newspapers.
PILLER *leaving:* You mean nothing to me. You mean nothing to literature.
All go.
SERVANT *entering:* Your coat, sir.

Baal's Attic

Starlit night. At the window Baal and the adolescent Johannes. They look at the sky.

BAAL: When you lie stretched out on the grass at night you

can feel in your bones that the earth is round and that we're flying, and that there are beasts on this star that devour its plants. It's one of the smaller stars.

JOHANNES: Do you know anything about astronomy?

BAAL: No.

Silence.

JOHANNES: I'm in love with a girl. She's the most innocent creature alive, but I saw her once in a dream being made love to by a juniper tree. That is to say, her white body lay stretched out on the juniper tree and the gnarled branches twisted about her. I haven't been able to sleep since.

BAAL: Have you ever seen her white body?

JOHANNES: No. She's innocent. Even her knees . . . There are degrees of innocence, don't you think? And yet, there are times when I hold her, just for a second, at night, and she trembles like a leaf, but only at night. But I haven't the strength to do it. She's seventeen.

BAAL: In your dream, did she like love?

JOHANNES: Yes.

BAAL: She wears clean linen, a snow-white petticoat between her knees? Bed her and she may turn into a heap of flesh without a face.

JOHANNES: You're saying what I always felt. I thought I was a coward. I can see now that you also think intercourse is unclean.

BAAL: That's the grunting of the swine who are no good at it. When you embrace her virginal loins, the joy and fear of created man turns you into a god. As the juniper tree's many roots are entwined within the earth, so are your limbs in bed. Blood flows and hearts beat.

JOHANNES: But it's punishable by law, and by one's parents.

BAAL: Your parents – *he reaches for his guitar* – they're a thing of the past. How dare they open their mouths, filled with rotten teeth, to speak against love, which anybody may die of? If you can't take love, there's nothing left but vomit. *He tunes the guitar.*

JOHANNES: Do you mean if I make her pregnant?

BAAL *striking chords on his guitar:* When the pale mild summer ebbs and they're swollen with love like sponges, they turn back into beasts, evil and childish, shapeless with their fat stomachs and hanging breasts, their damp arms clinging like slimy tentacles, and their bodies collapse and grow heavy unto death. And with hideous shrieks as if they were bringing a new world into being, they yield a small fruit. They spew out with pain what they once sucked in with pleasure. *He plucks the strings.* You have to have teeth for it, then love is like biting into an orange, with the juice squirting into your teeth.

JOHANNES: Your teeth are like an animal's. They're yellow and large, sinister.

BAAL: And love is like putting your naked arm into a pond and letting it float with weeds between your fingers, like the pain in which the drunken tree groans and sings as the wild wind rides it, like drowning in wine on a hot day, her body surging like a cool wine into every crease of your skin, limbs soft as plants in the wind, and the weight of the collision to which you yield is like flying against a storm, and her body tumbles over you like cool pebbles. But love is also like a coconut, good while it is fresh but when the juice is gone and only the bitter flesh remains you have to spit it out. *He throws the guitar aside.* I'm sick of this hymn.

JOHANNES: Then you think it's something I ought to do, if it's so wonderful?

BAAL: I think it's something for *you* to avoid, Johannes.

An Inn

Morning. Lorry-drivers. Ekart at the back with Luise, the waitress. White clouds can be seen through the window.

BAAL *talking to the lorry-drivers:* He threw me out of his nice clean room, because I threw up his wine. But his wife ran after me, and in the evening we celebrated. I'm lumbered with her and sick of it.

DRIVERS: She needs a good hiding . . . They're randy as cats but stupider. Tell her to go and eat figs! . . . I always beat mine before I give her what she wants.

JOHANNES *enters with Johanna:* This is Johanna.

BAAL *to the drivers, who go to the back:* I'll give you a song later.

JOHANNA: Johannes read me some of your poems.

BAAL: Ah. How old are you?

JOHANNES: She was seventeen in June.

JOHANNA: I'm jealous. He does nothing but talk about you.

BAAL: You're in love with your Johannes. It's spring. I'm waiting for Emilie . . . Better to love than make love.

JOHANNES: I can understand your winning a man's love, but how can you have any success with women?

Emilie enters quickly.

BAAL: Here she comes. And how are you, Emilie? Johannes is here with his fiancée. Sit down!

EMILIE: How could you ask me to come here! A cheap bar, only fit for drunken louts! Typical of your taste.

BAAL: Luise, a gin for the lady.

EMILIE: Do you want to make a laughing stock of me?

BAAL: No. You'll drink. We're all human.

EMILIE: But you're not.

BAAL: How do you know? *He holds the glass out to Luise.* Don't be so mean, Luise. *He takes hold of her.* You're devilishly soft today, like a plum.

EMILIE: How ill-bred you are!

BAAL: Tell the world, darling.

JOHANNES: It's interesting here, I must say. Ordinary people. Drinking and amusing themselves. And then, those clouds in the window!

EMILIE: He dragged you here too, I expect. For a view of the clouds.

JOHANNA: Wouldn't it be nicer to go for a walk in the meadows by the river, Johannes?

BAAL: Nothing doing! Stay here! *He drinks.* The sky is

purple, particularly if you happen to be drunk. Beds on the other hand are white. To begin with. That's where love is, between Heaven and Earth. *He drinks.* Why are you such cowards? The sky's free, you feeble shadows! Full of bodies! Pale with love!

EMILIE: You've had too much again and now you're babbling. And with that bloody wonderful babble he drags you to his sty.

BAAL: Sometimes – *drinks* – the sky is yellow. Full of vultures. Let's all get drunk. *He looks under the table.* Who's kicking my shins? Is it you, Luise? Ah, you, Emilie! Well, no matter. Drink up.

EMILIE *half rising:* I don't know what's wrong with you today. Perhaps I shouldn't have come here after all.

BAAL: Have you just noticed? You might as well stay now.

JOHANNA: Don't say things like that, Mr Baal.

BAAL: You've a good heart, Johanna. You'll never be unfaithful, will you?

DRIVER *winning:* Ace, you bastards! – Trumped!

SECOND DRIVER: Keep going, the tart said, the worst's over. *Laughter.* Tell her to go and eat figs.

THIRD DRIVER: How could you betray me, as the lady said to the butler when she found him in bed with the maid.

JOHANNES *to Baal:* Because of Johanna. She's a child.

JOHANNA *to Emilie:* Will you come with me? We can go together.

EMILIE *bursting into tears at the table:* I feel so ashamed now.

JOHANNA *putting her arm round Emilie:* I understand; it doesn't matter.

EMILIE: Don't look at me like that. You're still so young. You don't know anything yet.

BAAL *gets up forbiddingly:* Comedy, entitled Sisters in Hades! *He goes to the drivers, takes the guitar down from the wall and tunes it.*

JOHANNA: He's been drinking. He'll regret it tomorrow.

EMILIE: If only you knew. He's always like this. And I love him.

BAAL *sings:*

Orge told me that:

In all the world the place he liked the best
Was not the grass mound where his loved ones rest

Was not the altar, nor some harlot's room
Nor yet the warm white comfort of the womb.

Orge thought the best place known to man
In this world was the lavatory pan.

That was a place to set the cheeks aglow
With stars above and excrement below.

A place of refuge where you had a right
To sit in private on your wedding night.

A place of truth, for there you must admit
You are a man; there's no concealing it.

A place of wisdom, where the gut turns out
To gird itself up for another bout.

Where you are always doing good by stealth
Exerting tactful pressure for your health.

At that you realize how far you've gone:
Using the lavatory – to eat on.

DRIVERS *clapping:* Bravo! . . . A good song! Give the gentleman a cherry brandy, if you'll accept the offer, sir! He made it up all on his own . . . What a man!

LUISE *in the middle of the room:* You're a one, Mr Baal!

DRIVER: If *you* did a real job, you'd do all right for yourself. You could end up running a transport business.

SECOND DRIVER: Wish I had brains like that!

BAAL: That's nothing. You have to have a backside and the rest. Your very good health, Luise. *He goes back to his table.* And yours, Emmi. Come on, drink up. Even if you can't do anything else. Drink, I said.

Emilie, tears in her eyes, sips her drink.

BAAL: That's better. There'll be some life in you yet.

EKART *gets up and comes round slowly from the bar to Baal. He is lean, a powerful man:* Baal! Brother! Come with me! Give it up! Out to the hard dusty highroad: at night the air grows purple. To bars full of drunks: let the women you've stuffed fall into the black rivers. To cathedrals with small, pale ladies: you ask, dare a man breathe here? To cowsheds where you bed down with the beasts. It's dark there and the cows moo. And into the forests where axes ring out above and you forget the light of day: God has forgotten you. Do you still remember what the sky looks like? A fine tenor you've turned into! *He spreads his arms.* Come, brother! To dance, to sing, to drink! Rain to drench us! Sun to scorch us! Darkness and light! Dogs and women! Are you that degenerate?

BAAL: Luise! Luise! An anchor! Don't let me go with him. *Luise goes to him.* Help me, everyone.

JOHANNES: Don't let him lead you astray!

BAAL: My dear chap!

JOHANNES: Think of your mother, remember your art! Resist! *To Ekart:* You ought to be ashamed. You're evil.

EKART: Come, brother! We'll fly in the open sky as blissful as two white doves. Rivers in the morning light! Graveyards swept by the wind and the smell of endless unmown fields.

JOHANNA: Be strong, Mr Baal.

EMILIE *holding him:* I won't allow it! Do you hear? You can't throw yourself away!

BAAL: Not yet, Ekart! There's still another way. They won't play, brother.

EKART: Then go to the devil, you with your soft, fat, sentimental heart! *He goes.*

DRIVERS: Out with the ten . . . Damn it! Add up . . . Let's pack it in.

JOHANNA: You've won this time, Mr Baal.

BAAL: I'm sweating all over. Got any time today, Luise?

EMILIE: Don't talk like that, Baal! You don't know what you do to me when you talk like that.

LUISE: Stop upsetting the lady, Mr Baal. A child could see she's not herself.

BAAL: Don't worry, Luise! Horgauer!

DRIVER: What do you want?

BAAL: There's a lady being badly treated here, she wants love. Give her a kiss, Horgauer.

JOHANNES: Baal!

Johanna puts her arm round Emilie.

DRIVERS *laughing and hitting the table with their fists:* Press on, Andreas . . . Have a go . . . high class, blow your nose first . . . You're a bastard, Mr Baal.

BAAL: Are you frigid, Emilie? Do you love me? He's shy, Emmi. Give him a kiss. If you make a fool of me in front of these people, it's the finish. One, two . . .

The driver bends down. Emilie raises her tear-stained face. He kisses her vigorously. Loud laughter.

JOHANNES: That was evil, Baal. Drink brings out the evil in him, and then he feels good. He's too strong.

DRIVERS: Well done! What's she come to a place like this for? . . . That's the way to treat them . . . her kind break up families! . . . Serves her right! *They get up from their card game.* Tell her to go and eat figs!

JOHANNA: How disgusting! You ought to be ashamed!

BAAL *going up to her:* Why are your knees shaking, Johanna?

JOHANNES: What do you want with her?

BAAL *a hand on his shoulder:* Must you also write poetry? While life's so decent? When you shoot down a racing stream on your back, naked under an orange sky, and you see nothing except the sky turning purple, then black like a hole . . . when you trample your enemy underfoot . . . or burst with joy at a funeral . . . or sobbing with love you eat an apple . . . or bend a woman across a bed. *Johannes leads Johanna away without saying a word.*

BAAL *leaning on the table:* It's all a bloody circus. Did you feel it? Did it get under your skin? You have to lure the beast from its cage! Get the beast into the sun! My bill! Let love see the light of day! Naked in the sunshine! Under a clear sky!

DRIVERS *shaking him by the hand:* Be seeing you, Mr Baal! . . . At your service, sir! . . . For my part I always did say Mr Baal had a screw loose. What with those songs and the rest! But one thing's certain, his heart's in the right place! – You have to treat women the way they deserve. – Well, somebody exposed their precious white bottom here today. – Good-bye, Mr Circus. *They go.*

BAAL: And good-bye to you, my friends! *Emilie has thrown herself sobbing down on the bench. Baal touches her forehead with the back of his hand.* Emmi! You can calm down now. The worst is over. *He raises her head and brushes her hair from her tear-stained face.* Just forget it! *He throws himself heavily on her and kisses her.*

Baal's Attic

I *Sunrise.*
Baal and Johanna sitting on the edge of the bed.

JOHANNA: Oh, what have I done! I'm wicked.

BAAL: Wash yourself instead.

JOHANNA: I still don't know how it happened.

BAAL: Johannes is to blame for everything. Drags you up here and behaves like a clown when he sees why your knees are shaking.

JOHANNA *gets up, lowers her voice:* When he comes back . . .

BAAL: Time for a bit of literature. *He lies down again.* First light over Mount Ararat.

JOHANNA: Shall I get up?

BAAL: After the flood. Stay in bed.

JOHANNA: Won't you open the window?

BAAL: I like the smell. – What about another helping? What's gone's gone.

JOHANNA: How can you be so vile?

BAAL *lazily on the bed:* White and washed clean by the flood, Baal lets his thoughts fly like doves over the dark waters.

JOHANNA: Where's my petticoat . . . I can't . . . like this . . .

BAAL *handing it to her:* Here! What can't you . . . like this, darling?

JOHANNA: Go home. *She drops it, but then she dresses.*

BAAL *whistling:* God, what a girl! I can feel every bone in my body. Give me a kiss!

JOHANNA *by the table in the middle of the room:* Say something! *Baal is silent.* Do you still love me? Say it. *Baal whistles.* Can't you say it?

BAAL *looking up at the ceiling:* I'm fed to the teeth!

JOHANNA: Then what was it last night? And before?

BAAL: Johannes could make things awkward. And Emilie's staggering around like a rammed schooner. I could die of starvation here! None of you would lift a finger for me. There's only one thing you're out for.

JOHANNA *confused, clearing the table:* And you – didn't you ever feel differently about me?

BAAL: Have you washed? Not an ounce of sense. Did you get nothing out of it? Go home! You can tell Johannes I took you home last night and spew gall at him. It's been raining. *Rolls himself up in his blanket.*

JOHANNA: Johannes? *She walks wearily to the door and goes.*

BAAL *suddenly turning:* Johanna! *Goes from his bed to the door.* Johanna! *At the window.* There she goes. There she goes.

2 *Noon.*
Baal lies on his bed.

BAAL *humming:*

The evening sky grows dark as pitch
With drink; or often fiery red.
Naked I'll have you in a ditch . . .

The two sisters come into the room arm in arm.
THE OLDER SISTER: You said we were to come and visit you again.
BAAL *still humming:*

Or on a white and spacious bed.

THE OLDER SISTER: Well, we came, Mr Baal.
BAAL: Now they come fluttering in pairs to the dove-cot. Take off your clothes.
THE OLDER SISTER: Mother heard the stairs creak last week. *She undoes her sister's blouse.*
THE YOUNGER SISTER: It was getting light on the landing when we got to our room.
BAAL: One day I'll be stuck with you.
THE YOUNGER SISTER: I'd drown myself, Mr Baal.
THE OLDER SISTER: We came together . . .
THE YOUNGER SISTER: I feel ashamed.
THE OLDER SISTER: It isn't the first time . . .
THE YOUNGER SISTER: But it was never so light. It's broad daylight outside.
THE OLDER SISTER: And it isn't the second time.
THE YOUNGER SISTER: You get undressed as well.
THE OLDER SISTER: I will.
BAAL: When you've done, come on in! It'll be dark all right.
THE YOUNGER SISTER: You go first today.
THE OLDER SISTER: I was first last time . . .
THE YOUNGER SISTER: No, it was me . . .

BAAL: You'll both get it at once.

THE OLDER SISTER *standing with her arms round the younger one:* We're ready. It's so light in here!

BAAL: Is it warm outside?

THE OLDER SISTER: It's only April.

THE YOUNGER SISTER: But the sun's warm today.

BAAL: Did you enjoy yourselves last time?

The sisters do not answer.

THE OLDER SISTER: A girl threw herself into the river. Johanna Reiher.

THE YOUNGER SISTER: Into the Laach. I wouldn't go in there. The current's too strong.

BAAL: Into the river? Does anyone know why?

THE OLDER SISTER: There are rumours. People talk . . .

THE YOUNGER SISTER: She went off one afternoon and stayed out all night.

BAAL: Didn't she go home in the morning?

THE YOUNGER SISTER: No, then she went in the river. They haven't found her yet.

BAAL: Still afloat . . .

THE YOUNGER SISTER: What's the matter?

THE OLDER SISTER: Nothing. A chill perhaps.

BAAL: I'm too lazy today. You can go home.

THE OLDER SISTER: You can't do that, Mr Baal. You shouldn't do that to her.

Knocking at the door.

THE YOUNGER SISTER: Somebody's knocking. It's mother.

THE OLDER SISTER: For God's sake, don't open!

THE YOUNGER SISTER: I'm frightened.

THE OLDER SISTER: Here's your blouse.

Loud knocking.

BAAL: If it's your mother you're in for it.

THE OLDER SISTER *dressing quickly:* Wait a minute, don't open yet. Bolt the door, please, for God's sake!

LANDLADY *fat, enters:* Ah ha! I thought as much. Two at a time now! Aren't you ashamed of yourselves? A pair of you in his fishpond? Night and day, that fellow's bed never gets cold. Now I'm going to have my say. My attic isn't a brothel.

Baal turns to the wall.

LANDLADY: You're sleepy, are you? My word, don't you ever get enough of it? I can see the daylight through you. You look like a ghost. You're nothing but a bag of bones.

BAAL *moving his arms:* Like swans they fly to my wood.

LANDLADY *clapping her hands:* Nice swans! The way you put things! You could be a poet, you! If your knees don't rot first.

BAAL: I indulge in white bodies.

LANDLADY: White bodies! You're a poet, you really are! Don't know what else you are though. And the poor young things! You're sisters, are you? And snivelling because you're poor orphans, I suppose. How about a good hiding? For your white bodies? *Baal laughs.* And he laughs. You ruin poor girls by the hundredweight, poor girls you drag here. You disgusting pig! I'm giving you notice. As for you, look sharp and back to your mother! I'm coming with you.

The younger sister sobs loudly.

THE OLDER SISTER: It isn't her fault.

LANDLADY *taking both by the hand:* Now for the waterworks! These girls! Oh well, you're not the only ones. That one's up to his neck in swans. There's plenty besides you he's made happy, then dumped on the rubbish heap. Off with you now, into the fresh air! There's no need for tears. *She puts her arms round them both.* I know what he's like. I know the make. Stop snivelling, else it'll show in your eyes. Go home to your mother like good girls and don't do it again. *She pushes them out.* And you, you've had your notice. You can set up your swan-sty somewhere else. *She pushes the girls out of the room and goes out herself.*

BAAL *gets up, stretches:* A bitch with a heart! . . . I'm dead lazy today anyway. *He throws paper down on the table and sits down.* I'll make the new Adam. *He sketches big letters on the paper.* I'll have a go at the inner man. I'm hollowed out, but hungry as a vulture. Nothing but a bag of bones. The bitch! *He leans back and stretches his arms and legs with emphasis.* I'll make summer. Red. Scarlet red. Greedy. *He hums again.*

3 *Evening.*
Baal sits at his table.

BAAL *picks up the bottle. The following speech to be delivered with pauses:* I've covered the paper with red summer for four days now: wild, pale, greedy; and fought the bottle. There have been defeats, but the bodies on the wall are beginning to retreat into the dark, into the Egyptian night. I nail them to the wall, but I must stop drinking. *He murmurs:* This white liquor is my rod and staff. It reflects my paper and has remained untouched since the snow began to drip from the gutter. But now my hands are shaking. As if the bodies were still in them. *He listens.* My heart's pounding like a horse's hoof. *With enthusiasm:* Oh Johanna, one more night in your aquarium, and I would have rotted among the fish. But now I smell the warm May nights. I'm a lover with no one to love. I give in. *He drinks and gets up.* I must move. First I'll get myself a woman. To move out alone is sad. *He looks out of the window.* No matter who. One with a face like a woman. *Humming, he goes out. Tristan is being played down below on the hurdy gurdy.*
Johannes enters, wretched and pale. He riffles the papers on the table, picks up the bottle and goes shyly to the door.
He waits there.
Noise on the landing. Whistling.

BAAL *pulling Sophie Barger into the room. Whistles:* Be nice to me, darling. That is my room. *He sits down, sees Johannes.* What are you doing here?

JOHANNES: I only wanted to . . .

BAAL: So you wanted to? What are you standing there for? A tombstone for my Johanna, who's been washed away? The ghost of Johannes from another world, is that it? I'll throw you out! Leave this room at once! *Runs round him.* It's an impertinence! I'll knock you down. It's spring, anyway. Get out!

Johannes looks at him and goes.

Baal whistles.

SOPHIE: What did the poor boy do to you? Let me go!

BAAL *opens the door wide:* When you get to the first floor, turn to the right.

SOPHIE: They followed us after you picked me up in front of the door. They'll find me.

BAAL: No one will find you here.

SOPHIE: I don't even know you. What do you want from me?

BAAL: If you mean that, you may as well go.

SOPHIE: You rushed up to me in the street. I thought it was an orangutan.

BAAL: It's spring, isn't it? I need something white in this damned hole, a cloud. *He opens the door and listens.* Those idiots, they've lost their way.

SOPHIE: I'll get thrown out if I come home late.

BAAL: Especially —

SOPHIE: Especially what?

BAAL: The way a woman looks when I've made love to her.

SOPHIE: I don't know why I'm still here.

BAAL: I can give you the information.

SOPHIE: You needn't think the worst of me, please!

BAAL: Why not? You're a woman like any other. The faces vary, the knees are always weak.

Sophie is half prepared to go; at the door she looks round.

Baal looks at her, astride a chair.

SOPHIE: Good-bye!

BAAL *indifferently:* Do you feel faint?

SOPHIE *leans against the wall:* I don't know. I feel so weak.

BAAL: I know. It's April. It's growing dark, and you smell me. That's how it is with animals. *Gets up.* Now you belong to the wind, white cloud. *He goes to her quickly, slams the door, and takes Sophie Barger into his arms.*

SOPHIE *breathlessly:* Let me go!

BAAL: My name's Baal.

SOPHIE: Let me go!

BAAL: You must console me. The winter left me weak. And you look like a woman.

SOPHIE *looks up at him:* Your name's Baal?

BAAL: That makes you want to stay?

SOPHIE *looking up at him:* You're so ugly, so ugly, it's frightening. – But then —

BAAL: Mm?

SOPHIE: Then it doesn't matter.

BAAL *kisses her:* Are your knees steady, mm?

SOPHIE: You don't even know my name. I'm Sophie Barger.

BAAL: Forget your name. *Kisses her.*

SOPHIE: Don't – don't – it's the first time anybody's ever . . .

BAAL: Untouched? Come! *He leads her to the bed. They sit down.* You see! Bodies have poured through this room like water. But now I want a face. We'll go out tonight. We'll lie down in the fields. You're a woman. I've become unclean. You must love me, for a while.

SOPHIE: Is that what you're like? . . . I love you.

BAAL *rests his head on her breasts:* Now the sky's above us, and we're alone.

SOPHIE: But you must lie still.

BAAL: Like a child.

SOPHIE *sitting up:* My mother's at home. I have to go home.

BAAL: Is she old?

SOPHIE: She's seventy.

BAAL: Then she's used to wickedness.

SOPHIE: What if the earth swallowed me up? What if I'm carried off at night and never return?

BAAL: Never? *Silence.* Have you any brothers or sisters?

SOPHIE: Yes, they need me.

BAAL: The air here is like milk. *Goes to the window.* The willows down by the river are soaking wet, and unkempt from the rain. *Takes hold of her.* Your thighs must be pale.

Whitewashed Houses with Brown Tree Trunks

Sombre ringing of bells. Baal. The tramp, a pale drunk individual.

BAAL *striding in a half circle round the tramp, who sits on a stone, his pale face turned to the sky:* Who nailed the tree corpses to the wall?

TRAMP: The pale ivory wind around the corpses of trees. Corpus Christi.

BAAL: Not to mention ringing the bells when plants die!

TRAMP: Bells give me a moral uplift.

BAAL: Don't the trees depress you?

TRAMP: Pff! Tree carcases! *Drinks from a bottle.*

BAAL: Women's bodies aren't any better!

TRAMP: What have women's bodies to do with a religious procession?

BAAL: They're both obscene. There's no love in you.

TRAMP: There's love in me for the white body of Jesus. *Passes him the bottle.*

BAAL *calmer:* I wrote songs down on paper. They get hung up in lavatories these days.

TRAMP *transfigured:* To serve the Lord Jesus! I see the white body of Jesus. Jesus loves sinners.

BAAL *drinking:* Like me.

TRAMP: Do you know the story about him and the dead dog? They all said, it's a stinking mess. Fetch the police! It's unbearable! But, he said, it has nice white teeth.

BAAL: Perhaps I'll turn Catholic.

TRAMP: He didn't. *Takes the bottle from him.*

BAAL *runs about enraged:* But the women's bodies he nails to the wall. I wouldn't do that.

TRAMP: Nailed to the wall! They never floated down the river. They were slaughtered for him, for the white body of Jesus.

BAAL *takes the bottle from him, turns away:* There's too much religion or too much gin in your blood. *Walks away with the bottle.*

TRAMP *beside himself, shouting after him:* So you won't defend your ideals, sir! You won't join the procession? You love plants and won't do anything for them?

BAAL: I'm going down to the river to wash myself. I can't be bothered with corpses. *Goes.*

TRAMP: But I'm full of drink, I can't bear it. I can't bear the damned dead plants. If I had more gin in me, perhaps I could bear it.

Spring Night Beneath Trees

Baal. Sophie.

BAAL *lazily:* It's stopped raining. The grass must still be wet . . . it never came through the leaves of our tree. The young leaves are dripping wet, but here among the roots it's dry! *Angrily.* Why can't a man make love to a plant?

SOPHIE: Listen!

BAAL: The wild roaring of the wind through the damp, black foliage. Can you hear the rain drip from the leaves?

SOPHIE: I can feel a drop on my neck . . . Oh, let me go!

BAAL: Love rips the clothes from a man like a whirlpool and buries him naked among the corpses of leaves, after he's seen the sky.

SOPHIE: I should like to hide in you, Baal, because I'm naked.

BAAL: I'm drunk and you're staggering. The sky is black and we're on a swing with love in our bodies and the sky is black. I love you.

SOPHIE: Oh, Baal, my mother'll be weeping over my dead body, she'll think I drowned myself. How many weeks is it now? It wasn't even May then. It must be nearly three weeks.

BAAL: It must be nearly three weeks, said the beloved among the roots of the tree, after thirty years had passed and she was half rotted by then.

SOPHIE: It's good to lie here like a captive, with the sky above, and never be alone again.
BAAL: I'm going to take your petticoat off again.

A Club Called 'The Night Cloud'

A small, swinish café; whitewashed dressing-room; at the back on the left a dark brown curtain; to the side on the right a whitewashed door made of boards leading to the lavatory. At the back on the right a door. When it is open blue night sky is seen. A woman entertainer sings at the back of the café.
Baal walks around, chest and shoulders bare, drinking and humming. Lupu, a fat, pale boy with black glossy hair gummed down in two strips on to his sweaty, pale face and a prominent back to his head, stands in the doorway right.

LUPU: The lamp has been knocked down again.
BAAL: Only pigs come here. Where's my gin ration?
LUPU: You've drunk it all.
BAAL: You watch your step!
LUPU: Mjurk said something about a sponge.
BAAL: Does that mean I don't get a drink?
LUPU: No more gin for you until you've done your number, Mjurk said. I'm sorry for you.
MJURK *by the curtain:* Make yourself scarce, Lupu!
BAAL: No drink, no song.
MJURK: You shouldn't drink so much, or one of these days you won't be able to sing at all.
BAAL: Why else do I sing?
MJURK: Next to Savettka, you're the 'Night Cloud's' most brilliant attraction. You're my personal discovery. Was there ever such a delicate talent in such a fat lump? The fat lump makes the success, not the songs. Your drinking'll ruin me.
BAAL: I'm sick of haggling every night for gin that's my contractual right. I'm clearing out.

MJURK: I've got police backing. You should try sleeping one of these nights, you crawl around as if you'd been hamstrung. Tell your sweetheart to go to hell! *Applause in the café.* You're on now, anyway.

BAAL: I'm fed to the teeth.

Savettka with the pianist, a pale apathetic individual, coming from behind the curtain:

SAVETTKA: That's my lot. I'm off now.

MJURK *forcing a tail-coat on Baal:* You don't go half naked on to the stage in my club.

BAAL: Moron! *He throws down the tail-coat and goes off behind the curtain, dragging the guitar.*

SAVETTKA *sits down and drinks:* He only works for that woman he's living with. He's a genius. Lupu imitates him shamelessly. He has taken his tone as well as his girl.

PIANIST *leaning on the lavatory door:* His songs are divine but he's been haggling with Lupu for his drink for the last ten days.

SAVETTKA *drinking:* Life's hell!

BAAL *from behind the curtain:* Small am I, pure am I, a jolly little boy am I. *Applause. Baal continues, accompanying himself on the guitar:*

Through the room the wild wind comes.
What's the child been eating? Plums.
Soft and white its body lay
Helping pass the time away.

Applause and whistles. Baal goes on singing, and the noise gets rowdier as the song gets more and more shameless. Finally, uproar in the café.

PIANIST *phlegmatically:* My God, he's packing up. Call a doctor! Now Mjurk's talking, they'll tear him to pieces. No one censored that!

Baal comes from behind the curtain, dragging his guitar.

MJURK *following him:* You bastard! I'll have the hide off you!

You are going to sing! As stated in the contract! Or I'll get the police. *He goes back behind the curtain.*

PIANIST: You'll ruin us, Baal.

Baal raises a hand to his throat and goes to the lavatory door.

PIANIST *not letting him pass:* Where are you off to?

Baal pushes him aside and goes through the door, dragging his guitar after him.

SAVETTKA: Taking your guitar to the lavatory? Lovely!

GUESTS *peering in:* Where's that bastard? Go on with the song – don't stop now! The filthy bastard! *They return to the room.*

MJURK: I spoke like a Salvation Army general. We can rely on the police. But they're shouting for him again. Where is he? He'll have to go on.

PIANIST: The main attraction's sitting on the lavatory.

Cry from behind the scenes: Baal!

MJURK *drumming on the door:* You. Answer me! Damn it, I forbid you to lock yourself in! While I'm paying you! I've got it in writing. You swindler! *Thumps wildly.*

LUPU *in the door on the right. Blue night sky outside:* The lavatory window's open. The bird has flown. No drink, no song!

MJURK: Empty! Gone? Out through the lavatory? The cutthroat! Police! I want the police! *He rushes out. Calls in rhythm from behind the curtain: Baal! Baal! Baal!*

Green Fields. Blue Plum Trees

Baal. Ekart.

BAAL *slowly coming through the fields:* Since the sky turned green and pregnant, summertime, wind, no shirt in my trousers. *Back to Ekart.* They rub my backside, my skull's blown up with the wind, and the smell of the fields hangs in the hair of my armpits. The air trembles as if it were drunk.

EKART *behind him:* Why are you running away from the plum trees like an elephant?

BAAL: Put your hand on my head. It swells with every pulse-beat and goes down like a balloon. Can't you feel it?

EKART: No.

BAAL: You don't understand my soul.

EKART: Let's go and lie in the river.

BAAL: My soul, brother, is the groaning of the cornfields as they bend in the wind, and the gleam in the eyes of two insects who want to devour each other.

EKART: A mad summer boy with immortal intestines, that's what you are! A dumpling, who'll leave a grease spot on the sky.

BAAL: Only words. But it doesn't matter.

EKART: My body's light as a little plum in the wind.

BAAL: That's because of the pale summer sky, brother. Shall we soak up the warm water of a blue pond? Otherwise the white roads that lead across the land will draw us like angels' ropes up to heaven.

Village Inn

Evening. Farmers. Baal. Ekart on his own in a corner.

BAAL: I'm glad I've got you all here together. My brother will be here tomorrow evening. The bulls have to be here by then.

FARMER *gaping:* How can we see if a bull's the right sort for your brother?

BAAL: Only my brother can see. They all have to be strong, fine beasts. Or they're no use. Another gin!

SECOND FARMER: Will you buy the bull on the spot?

BAAL: The one with the strongest legs.

THIRD FARMER: For your price they'll bring them from eleven villages.

FIRST FARMER: Come and have a look at *my* bull.

BAAL: A gin!

FARMERS: My bull is the best! Tomorrow evening, you said? *They separate.* – Are you staying the night here?

BAAL: Yes, in a bed.

The farmers go.

EKART: What are you trying to do? Have you gone mad?

BAAL: Wasn't it wonderful, the way they gawped and gaped, and then they got the idea and began to add up.

EKART: It brought in a few gins! But now we'd better get out quickly.

BAAL: Go now? Are you mad?

EKART: You're crazy! Think of the bulls!

BAAL: And just why did I jockey the boys?

EKART: Well – for the drinks?

BAAL: Wake up! I wanted to give you a treat, Ekart. *He opens the window behind him. It grows dark. He sits down again.*

EKART: You're drunk on six gins. You should be ashamed.

BAAL: It's going to be tremendous. I love these simple people. You're going to see an impressive sight, Ekart. Your health!

EKART: You love pretending to be more naïve than you are. Those poor fellows will beat me up – and you.

BAAL: It'll be part of their education. I'm thinking about them now on this warm evening with a certain tenderness. They come, in their own simple way, to swindle, and that pleases me.

EKART: All right, the bulls or me! I'm going, before the landlord catches on.

BAAL: The evening is so warm. Stay another hour. Then I'll go with you. You know I love you. One can even smell the dung on the fields from here. Do you think the landlord would stand the promoters of the bull business another gin?

EKART: There's someone coming!

PARSON *enters:* Good evening! Are you the man with the bulls?

BAAL: I am.

PARSON: What is the object of this hoax?

BAAL: Because we have nothing else in the world! How strong the smell of the hay is! Is it always like this in the evenings?

PARSON: Your world seems to be very impoverished, my friend.

BAAL: My heaven is full of trees and naked bodies.

PARSON: Don't talk like that. The world isn't a circus for your entertainment.

BAAL: What is the world, then?

PARSON: Just clear out. I'm a very good-natured person, you know. I don't want to make things difficult for you. I've dealt with the matter.

BAAL: The man of God has no sense of humour, Ekart.

PARSON: Don't you realize how childish your plan was? *To Ekart:* What does your friend want?

BAAL *leaning back:* In the evening when it gets dark – of course, it has to be evening and of course the sky must be cloudy – when the air is warm and the wind gentle, the bulls come. They come trotting from every direction, an impressive sight. And the poor farmers stand in the middle and don't know what to do with the bulls, and they've miscalculated: all they get is an impressive sight. I like people who miscalculate. And where else can you see so many animals together?

PARSON: And just for this you wanted to mobilize seven villages?

BAAL: What are seven villages compared with an impressive sight?

PARSON: Now I understand. You're just a poor fellow. With a particular liking for bulls, I suppose?

BAAL: Come, Ekart, he's spoilt it all. Christians don't love animals any more.

PARSON *laughs, then seriously:* I can't agree with you there. Be off now, and don't make yourselves conspicuous. I think I'm rendering you a considerable service.

BAAL: Let's go, Ekart. You've missed your treat, brother. *He slowly leaves with Ekart.*

PARSON: Good evening! I'll settle the gentlemen's bill.

LANDLORD *behind the table:* Eleven gins, your reverence.

Trees in the Evening

Six or seven woodcutters are sitting on the ground leaning against a tree, among them Baal. A corpse in the grass.

FIRST WOODCUTTER: It was an oak tree. It didn't kill him at once. He suffered.

SECOND WOODCUTTER: Only this morning he said the weather seemed to be getting better. This is how he liked it, green and a bit of rain. And the wood not too dry.

THIRD WOODCUTTER: He was a good lad, Teddy. He used to keep a small shop somewhere. In the old days. Used to be as fat as a priest. He ruined his business on account of a woman, and he came up here. Lost a bit of his paunch every year.

ANOTHER WOODCUTTER: Didn't he ever say anything about the woman?

THIRD WOODCUTTER: No. And I don't know that he wanted to go back. He saved quite a bit, but maybe that was because he was abstemious. Nobody tells the truth up here. It's better that way.

A WOODCUTTER: Last week he said he was going north this winter. It seems he had a cabin somewhere up there. Didn't he tell you where, elephant? *To Baal:* You were talking about it, weren't you?

BAAL: Leave me alone. I don't know anything.

THE PREVIOUS ONE: You wouldn't be thinking of moving in yourself, eh?

SECOND WOODCUTTER: You can't trust that one. Remember how he put our boots in the water that night, so we couldn't go to the forest the next day. Only because he was lazy as usual.

ANOTHER WOODCUTTER: He does nothing for his money.

BAAL: It's not a day for wrangling. Can't you spare a thought for poor Teddy?

A WOODCUTTER: Where were you when he packed in?

Baal gets up, sways over the grass to Teddy. He sits there.

THE PREVIOUS ONE: Look, he can't walk straight!

ANOTHER: Leave him alone! The elephant had a shock!

THE THIRD: Can't you keep it quiet just for today while he's lying there.

THE OTHER: What are you doing to Teddy, elephant?

BAAL *by the corpse:* Teddy is at peace, and we are the opposite. Both are good. The sky is black. The trees shudder. Somewhere clouds gather. That is the setting. One eats. After sleep one wakes. Not him. Us. And that's doubly good.

THE OTHER: What did you say the sky was like?

BAAL: The sky is black.

THE OTHER: You're not all there. The good ones always cop it first.

BAAL: How right you are, my dear chap!

A WOODCUTTER: It couldn't happen to Baal. He's never around where there's work.

BAAL: But Teddy, he was a hard worker. Teddy was generous. Teddy was friendly. One thing's certain: Teddy *was.*

THE SECOND: Wonder where he is now?

BAAL *points to the dead man:* There he is.

THE THIRD: I always get the feeling that the wind is made of dead souls, especially on spring evenings. But I get the feeling in autumn too.

BAAL: And in summer, in the sun, over the cornfields.

THE THIRD: That doesn't fit. It has to be dark.

BAAL: It has to be dark, Teddy.

Silence.

FOURTH WOODCUTTER: What are we going to do with him?

THE THIRD: He's got nobody who wants him.

THE OTHER: He was just on his own in the world.

A WOODCUTTER: What about his things?

THE THIRD: There isn't much. He carried his money off somewhere, to a bank. It'll stay there even if he doesn't turn up. Got any idea, Baal?

BAAL: He doesn't stink yet.

A WOODCUTTER: I've just had a good idea.

THE OTHER: Out with it!

THE MAN WITH THE IDEA: The elephant's not the only one with ideas, mate. What about drinking Teddy's good health?

BAAL: That's indecent, Bergmeier.

THE OTHERS: Rot, indecent. What shall we drink? Water? What a lousy idea!

THE MAN WITH THE IDEA: Gin!

BAAL: I vote in favour. Gin is decent. Whose gin?

THE MAN WITH THE IDEA: Teddy's gin.

THE OTHERS: Teddy's! – Sounds all right. – Teddy's ration! – Teddy was careful. – Not a bad idea for an idiot.

THE MAN WITH THE IDEA: A brainwave, what! Something for you blockheads! Teddy's gin at Teddy's funeral! Cheap and fitting! Anybody made a speech yet? Isn't that the proper thing to do?

BAAL: I did.

SOME: When?

BAAL: Earlier. Before you began to talk rubbish. It began with 'Teddy is at peace' . . . You don't notice anything until it's over.

THE OTHERS: Blockhead! Let's get the gin!

BAAL: It's a disgrace!

THE OTHERS: Oho! – Why, you big elephant.

BAAL: It's Teddy's property. The bottles must not be opened. Teddy's got a wife and five poor orphans.

A WOODCUTTER: Four! Four orphans!

ANOTHER: It's all coming out now.

BAAL: Do you want to drink the gin that belongs to Teddy's five poor orphans? Is that Christian?

THE PREVIOUS ONE: Four! Four orphans!

BAAL: Taking gin out of the mouths of Teddy's four orphans.

A WOODCUTTER: Teddy hasn't any family at all.

BAAL: But orphans, my friend, orphans.

ANOTHER: Do you think these orphans the elephant keeps

kidding you about are going to drink Teddy's gin? All right, it's Teddy's property . . .

BAAL *interrupts:* It was . . .

THE OTHER: What are you getting at?

A WOODCUTTER: He's jabbering. He's not all there.

THE OTHER: As I said, it was Teddy's property and so we'll pay for it. In cash. That'll fix the orphans.

EVERYBODY: A good suggestion. So much for the elephant. He must be mad, not to want any gin. Let's leave him and get Teddy's drink!

BAAL *calls after them:* Come back, you bloody scavengers! *To Teddy:* Poor Teddy! And the trees are pretty strong today and the air is good and soft, and I feel fortified within. Poor Teddy, don't you feel a tickle? You're through, I'm telling you, soon you'll stink, and everything will go on as before, the wind will blow, and I know where your cabin is, and your property will be taken over by the living, and you abandoned it and only wanted peace. Your body wasn't so bad, Teddy, it isn't so bad now, only a little damaged on one side and the legs . . . it would have finished you with women, you can't put that on top of a woman. *He lifts the dead man's leg.* With a bit more luck you could have gone on living, though, in that body, but your soul was too bloody choosy, the building was condemned, and the rats left the sinking ship. You were just a victim of your own habits, Teddy.

THE OTHERS *returning:* Hey, elephant! You're in for it! Where's the gin Teddy kept under his old bed? – Where were you when we were looking after Teddy? Teddy wasn't even dead then. – Where were you then, you son of a bitch, robbing the dead, protecting Teddy's poor orphans, eh?

BAAL: You've got no proof, my friends!

THE OTHERS: Where's the gin, then? In your esteemed opinion, did the bottle drink it? – This is a serious matter, old chap! – Stand up, you, get up! Walk in a straight line and then try and tell us it's the shock, it's because you're completely rotten, body and soul, you swine! – Get him on his legs! Liven him up, boys. Besmirching Teddy's poor old name! *They put Baal on his feet.*

BAAL: Bastards! Don't trample on poor Teddy! *He sits down and takes the arm of the corpse under his arm.* If you do anything to me, Teddy'll fall flat on his face. Is that piety? Anything I do will be in self-defence. There are seven of you, seven, and sober. And I'm on my own and drunk. Is that right, is that honourable? Seven against one! Calm down! Teddy's calmed down.

SOME *sad and indignant:* Nothing's sacred to him. – God forgive his drunken soul! – He's the blackest sinner on God's earth.

BAAL: Sit down, I don't like this preacher's cant. There are some with brains and some without. It makes for a better division of labour. Now you've seen for yourselves. I work with my brains. *He smokes.* You've always been too irreverent, friends! And what effect would it have if you sank that good gin? Me, I make discoveries, let me say. I was telling Teddy some most important things. *He takes papers from Teddy's jacket and looks at them.* But you had to run after that wretched gin. Sit down. Look at the sky growing dark between the trees. Is that nothing? There's no religion in your blood!

A Hut

You can hear the rain. Baal. Ekart.

BAAL: This is the winter sleep of white bodies in the black mud.

EKART: You still haven't been to fetch the meat?

BAAL: You're working on your mass, I suppose?

EKART: Why worry about my mass? Worry about your woman! Where have you driven her to this time, in the rain?

BAAL: She runs after us like a mad woman and hangs round my neck.

EKART: You're sinking lower and lower.

BAAL: I'm too heavy.

EKART: You're not reckoning to peg out, I suppose?

BAAL: I'll fight it to the last ditch. I'll live without a skin. I'll retreat into my toes. I'll fall like a bull. On the grass, where it's softest. I'll swallow death and know nothing.

EKART: You've got fatter while we've been lying here.

BAAL *putting his right hand under his left armpit:* My shirt has got bigger. The dirtier it gets the bigger it gets. There's room for someone else, but no one fat. What are you lolling about for, you lazy bag of bones?

EKART: There's a kind of sky in my head, very green and vast, where my thoughts drift like featherweight clouds in the wind. They're completely undecided in their course. All that's inside me.

BAAL: It's delirium. You're an alcoholic. You see, it gets you in the end.

EKART: When I'm delirious I can feel it by my face.

BAAL: Your face has room for the four winds. Concave! *He looks at him.* You haven't a face. You're nothing. You're transparent.

EKART: I'm growing more and more mathematical.

BAAL: Nobody knows your history. Why don't you ever talk about yourself?

EKART: I shan't ever have one. Who's that outside?

BAAL: You've got a good ear! There's something in you that you hide. You're a bad man, like me, a devil. But one day you'll see rats. Then you'll be a good man again.

Sophie at the door.

EKART: Is that you, Sophie?

BAAL: What do you want this time?

SOPHIE: May I come in now, Baal?

A Plain. Sky

Evening. Baal, Ekart, Sophie.

SOPHIE: My knees are giving way. Why are you running like a mad man?
BAAL: Because you're hanging round my neck like a millstone.
EKART: How can you treat her like this? You made her pregnant.
SOPHIE: I wanted it, Ekart.
BAAL: She wanted it, and now she's hanging round my neck.
EKART: You behave like an animal! Sit down, Sophie.
SOPHIE *sits down heavily:* Let him go.
EKART: If you throw her out I'll stay with her.
BAAL: She won't stay with you. But you'd desert me! Because of her? That's like you.
EKART: Twice you took my place in bed. You didn't want my women. They left you cold, but you stole them from me although I loved them.
BAAL: Because you loved them. Twice I defiled corpses to keep you clean. I need that. God knows, it gave me no pleasure.
EKART *to Sophie:* Are you still in love with this depraved animal?
SOPHIE: I can't help it, Ekart. I'd love his corpse. I even love his fists. I can't help it, Ekart.
BAAL: Don't ever tell me what you two were up to while I was inside!
SOPHIE: We stood together in front of the white prison wall and looked up at your window.
BAAL: You were together.
SOPHIE: Beat me for it.
EKART *shouts:* Didn't you throw her at me?
BAAL: You might have been stolen from me.
EKART: I haven't got your elephant's hide.

BAAL: I love you for it.

EKART: Keep your damned mouth shut about it while she's still with us!

BAAL: Tell her to get lost! She's turning into a bitch! *He puts his hands up to his throat.* She's washing her dirty laundry in your tears. Can you still not see that she's running naked between us? I have the patience of a lamb, but I can't change my skin.

EKART *sits down beside Sophie:* Go home to your mother.

SOPHIE: I can't.

BAAL: She can't, Ekart.

SOPHIE: Beat me if you want, Baal. I won't ask you to walk slowly again. I didn't mean to. Let me keep up with you, as long as I can. Then I'll lie down in the bushes and you needn't look. Don't drive me away, Baal.

BAAL: Throw your fat body into the river. I'm sick of you, and it's your own doing.

SOPHIE: Do you want to leave me here or don't you? You're still uncertain, Baal. You're like a child, to talk like that.

BAAL: I'm fed to the teeth with you.

SOPHIE: But not at night, Baal, not at night! I'm afraid alone. I'm afraid of the dark. I'm frightened of it.

BAAL: In your condition? No one will touch you.

SOPHIE: But tonight! Just wait both of you tonight.

BAAL: Go to the bargemen! It's midsummer night. They'll be drunk.

SOPHIE: A few minutes!

BAAL: Come on, Ekart!

SOPHIE: Where shall I go?

BAAL: To heaven, darling!

SOPHIE: With my child?

BAAL: Bury it.

SOPHIE: I pray that you'll never have cause to remember what you've just said to me, under this beautiful sky you love. I pray for it on my knees.

EKART: I'll stay with you. And then I'll take you to your mother, if you say you'll stop loving this swine.

BAAL: She loves me.
SOPHIE: I love him.
EKART: Are you still on your feet, you swine! Haven't you got knees? Are you besotted with drink or poetry? Depraved swine! Depraved swine!
BAAL: Simpleton.
Ekart attacks him, they fight.
SOPHIE: Mother of God! They're like wild animals!
EKART *fighting:* Did you hear what she said? Back there! And it's getting dark now. Depraved animal! Depraved animal!
BAAL *against him, pressing Ekart to himself:* Now you're close to me. Can you smell me? Now I'm holding you. There's more than the closeness of women. *He stops.* Look, you can see the stars above the trees now, Ekart.
EKART *looks hard at Baal, who gazes up into the sky:* I can't strike this thing!
BAAL *his arm round Ekart:* It's getting dark. We must find a place for the night. There are hollows in the wood where the wind never penetrates. Come, I'll tell you about the animals. *He draws him away.*
SOPHIE *alone in the dark, screams:* Baal!

Brown Wooden Bar

Night. Wind. At tables, Gougou, Bolleboll. The old beggar and Maja with a child in a box.

BOLLEBOLL *playing cards with Gougou:* I've no more money. Let's play for our souls.
THE BEGGAR: Brother wind wants to come in. But we don't know our cold brother wind. Heh, heh, heh!
The child cries.
MAJA *the beggar woman:* Listen! Something's prowling round the house. Pray God it's no wild beast!
BOLLEBOLL: Why? Are you feeling randy again?
Knocking at the door.

MAJA: Listen! I won't open.
THE BEGGAR: You will open.
MAJA: No, no, Mother of God, no!
THE BEGGAR: Bouque la Madonne! Open up!
MAJA *crawls to the door:* Who's outside?
The child cries. Maja opens the door.
BAAL *enters with Ekart, soaked to the skin:* Is this where they look after the sick?
MAJA: Yes, but there's no bed free. *More insolently:* And I'm ill.
BAAL: We've brought champagne. *Ekart has gone to warm himself by the stove.*
BOLLEBOLL: Come here! The man who knows what champagne is, is good enough for us.
THE BEGGAR: There's high society here today, my boy!
BAAL *goes up to the table and pulls two bottles from his pocket:* Mmm?
THE BEGGAR: That's fishy.
BOLLEBOLL: I know where you got that champagne. But I won't give you away.
BAAL: Here, Ekart! Any glasses?
MAJA: Cups, kind gentlemen. Cups. *She brings some.*
GOUGOU: I need a cup of my own.
BAAL *doubtful:* Are you allowed to drink champagne?
GOUGOU: Please! *Baal pours him some.*
BAAL: What's wrong with you?
GOUGOU: Bronchitis. Nothing bad. A little inflammation. Nothing serious.
BAAL *to Bolleboll:* And you?
BOLLEBOLL: Stomach ulcers. Won't kill me!
BAAL *to the beggar:* There's something wrong with you too, I trust?
THE BEGGAR: I'm mad.
BAAL: Here's to you! We understand each other. I'm healthy.
THE BEGGAR: I knew a man who said he was healthy too. He believed it. He came from the forest and one day he

went back there as there was something he had to think over. He found the forest very strange and no longer familiar, he walked for many days. Always deeper into the forest, because he wanted to see how independent he was and how much endurance there was left in him. But there wasn't much. *He drinks.*

BAAL *uneasy:* What a wind! We have to move on tonight, Ekart.

THE BEGGAR: Yes, the wind. One evening, at sunset, when he was no longer alone, he went through the great stillness between the trees and stood beneath one of the highest. *Drinks.*

BOLLEBOLL: That was the ape in him.

THE BEGGAR: Yes, perhaps it was the ape. He leant against it, very closely, and felt the life in it, or thought so. And he said, you are higher than I am and stand firm and you know the earth beneath you, and it holds you. I can run and move better, but I do not stand firm and I do not reach into the depths of the earth and nothing holds me up. Nor do I know the quiet of the endless sky above the still tree-tops. *He drinks.*

GOUGOU: What did the tree say?

THE BEGGAR: Yes. And the wind blew. A shudder ran through the tree. And the man felt it. He threw himself down on the ground and he clutched the wild, hard roots and cried bitterly. But he did it to many trees.

EKART: Did it cure him?

THE BEGGAR: No. He had an easier death, though.

MAJA: I don't understand that.

THE BEGGAR: Nothing is understood. But some things are felt. If one understands a story it's just that it's been told badly.

BOLLEBOLL: Do you believe in God?

BAAL *with an effort:* I've always believed in myself. But a man *could* turn atheist.

BOLLEBOLL *laughs loudly:* Now I feel happy. God! Champagne! Love! Wind and rain! *He reaches for Maja.*

MAJA: Leave me alone. Your breath stinks.

BOLLEBOLL: And I suppose you haven't got the pox? *He takes her on his lap.*

THE BEGGAR: Watch it! *To Bolleboll:* I'm getting drunker and drunker. If I get completely drunk you can't go out in the rain tonight.

GOUGOU *to Ekart:* He used to be better looking, that's how he got her.

EKART: What about your intellectual superiority? Your psychic ascendancy?

GOUGOU: She wasn't like that. She was completely innocent.

EKART: And what did you do?

GOUGOU: I was ashamed.

BOLLEBOLL: Listen! The wind. It's asking God for peace.

MAJA *sings:*

Lullaby baby, away from the storm
Here we are sheltered and drunken and warm.

BAAL: Whose child is that?

MAJA: My daughter, sir.

THE BEGGAR: A virgo dolorosa.

BAAL *drinks:* That's how it used to be, Ekart. And it was all right too.

EKART: What?

BOLLEBOLL: He's forgotten what.

BAAL: Used to be! That's a strange phrase!

GOUGOU *to Ekart:* The best of all is nothingness.

BOLLEBOLL: Pst! We're going to have Gougou's aria. A song from the old bag of worms.

GOUGOU: It's as if the air was quivering on a summer evening. Sunshine. But it isn't quivering. Nothing. Nothing at all. You just stop. The wind blows, and you don't feel cold. It rains, and you don't get wet. Funny things happen, and you don't laugh with the others. You rot, and you don't need to wait. General strike.

THE BEGGAR: That's Hell's Paradise.

GOUGOU: Yes, that's paradise. No wish unfulfilled. You have none left. You learn to abandon all your habits. Even wishing. That's how you become free.

MAJA: What happened in the end?

GOUGOU *grins:* Nothing. Nothing at all. There is no end. Nothingness lasts for ever.

BOLLEBOLL: Amen.

BAAL *gets up, to Ekart:* Ekart, get up. We've fallen among murderers. *He supports himself by putting his arm round Ekart's shoulders.* The vermin multiply. The rot sets in. The maggots sing and show off.

EKART: It's the second time that's happened to you. I wonder if it's just the drink.

BAAL: My guts are hanging out . . . this is no mud bath.

EKART: Sit down. Get drunk. Warm yourself.

MAJA *drunk, sings:*

Summer and winter and snowstorms and rain
If we aren't sober we won't feel the pain.

BOLLEBOLL *takes hold of Maja and pummels her:* Your aria tickles me, little Gougou. Itsiwitsi, little Maja.

The child cries.

BAAL *drinks:* Who are you? *Amused, to Gougou:* Your name's bag of worms. Are you a candidate for the mortuary? Your health! *He sits down.*

THE BEGGAR: Watch out, Bolleboll! Champagne doesn't agree with me.

MAJA *hanging on to Bolleboll, sings:*

Seeing is suffering, keep your eyes shut
All go to sleep now, and nothing will hurt.

BAAL *brutally:*

Float down the river with rats in your hair
Everything's lovely, the sky is still there.

He gets up, glass in hand. The sky is black! Did that scare you? *Drums on the table.* You have to stand the roundabout. It's wonderful. *He sways.* I want to be an elephant in a circus and pee when things go wrong . . . *He begins to dance and sing.* Dance with the wind, poor corpse! Sleep with a cloud, you degenerate God! *He goes up to the table, swaying.*

EKART *gets up, drunk:* I'm not going with you any farther. I've got a soul too. You corrupted my soul. You corrupt everything. And then I shall start on my Mass again.

BAAL: Your health! I love you.

EKART: But I'm not going with you any farther. *He sits down.*

THE BEGGAR *to Bolleboll:* Hands off, you pig!

MAJA: What's it got to do with you?

THE BEGGAR: Shut up, you poor thing!

MAJA: You're raving!

BOLLEBOLL *venomously:* He's a fraud. There's nothing wrong with him. That's right. It's all a fraud!

THE BEGGAR: And you've got cancer.

BOLLEBOLL *uncannily quiet:* I've got cancer?

THE BEGGAR *turning coward:* I didn't say anything. Leave her alone! *Maja laughs.*

BAAL: Why's it crying? *Sways to the box.*

THE BEGGAR *angry:* What do you want?

BAAL *leans over the box:* Why are you crying? Have you never seen them at it before? Or do you cry every time?

THE BEGGAR: Leave it alone, you! *He throws his glass at Baal.*

MAJA: You pig!

BOLLEBOLL: He's only having a peep under her skirt!

BAAL *gets up slowly:* Oh you swine! You don't know what's human any more. Come on, Ekart! We'll wash ourselves in the river. *He leaves with Ekart.*

Green Thicket. River Beyond

Baal. Ekart.

BAAL *sitting in the thicket:* The water's warm. You can lie like a crab on the sand. And the shrubs and white clouds in the sky. Ekart!
EKART *concealed:* What do you want?
BAAL: I love you.
EKART: I'm too comfortable here.
BAAL: Did you see the clouds earlier?
EKART: Yes, they're shameless. *Silence.* A while ago a woman went by on the other side.
BAAL: I don't care for women any longer . . .

Country Road. Willows

Wind. Night. Ekart asleep in the grass. Baal comes across the fields as if drunk, his clothes open, like a sleepwalker.

BAAL: Ekart! Ekart! I've got it! Wake up!
EKART: What's the matter? Are you talking in your sleep again?
BAAL *sits down by him:* This:

When she had drowned, and started her slow descent
Down the streams to where the rivers broaden
The opal sky shone most magnificent
As if it had to be her body's guardian.

Wrack and seaweed cling to her as she swims
Slowly their burden adds to her weight.
Coolly fishes play about her limbs
Creatures and growths encumber her in her final state.

And in the evening the sky grew dark as smoke
And at night the stars kept the light still soaring.
But soon it cleared as dawn again broke
To preserve her sequence of evening and morning.

As her pale body decayed in the water there
It happened (very slowly) that God gradually forgot it
First her face, then the hands, and right at the last her hair
Then she rotted in rivers where much else rotted.

The wind.

EKART: Has the ghost risen? It's not as wicked as you. Now sleep's gone to the devil and the wind is groaning in the willows like an organ. Nothing left but the white breast of philosophy, darkness, cold, and rain right up to our blessed end, and even for old women nothing left but their second sight.

BAAL: You don't need gin to be drunk in this wind. I see the world in a soft light: it is the excrement of the Almighty.

EKART: The Almighty, who made himself known once and for all through the association of the urinary passage with the sexual organ.

BAAL *lying down:* It's all so beautiful.

Wind.

EKART: The willows are like rotten teeth in the black mouth of the sky. I shall start work on my Mass soon.

BAAL: Is the quartet finished?

EKART: When did I have the time?

Wind.

BAAL: It's that redhead, the pale one, that you drag everywhere.

EKART: She has a soft white body, and at noon she brings it with her under the willows. They've drooping branches like hair, behind which we fuck like squirrels.

BAAL: Is she more beautiful than me?

Darkness. The wind blows on.

Young Hazel Shrubs

Long red switches hanging down. In the middle of them, Baal, sitting. Noon.

BAAL: I'll satisfy her, the white dove . . . *He looks at the place.* You get a good view of the clouds here through the willow . . . when he comes there'll only be skin left. I'm sick of his love affairs. Be calm!

A young woman comes out of the thicket. Red hair, a full figure.

BAAL *without looking round:* Is that you?

THE YOUNG WOMAN: Where's your friend?

BAAL: He's doing a Mass in E flat minor.

THE YOUNG WOMAN: Tell him I was here.

BAAL: He's too thin. He's transparent. He defiles himself. He's regressing into zoology. Do sit down! *He looks round.*

THE YOUNG WOMAN: I prefer to stand.

BAAL: He's been eating too many eggs lately. *He pulls himself up by the red switches.*

THE YOUNG WOMAN: I love him.

BAAL: You're no concern of mine. *He takes her in his arms.*

THE YOUNG WOMAN: Don't touch me! You're too dirty!

BAAL *slowly reaches for her throat:* Is that your throat? Do you know how they put down pigeons, or wild ducks in the wood?

THE YOUNG WOMAN: Mother of God! Leave me alone! *She struggles.*

BAAL: With your weak knees? You're falling over already. You want to be laid in the willows. A man's a man, in this respect most of them are equal. *He takes her in his arms.*

THE YOUNG WOMAN *shaking:* Please, let me go!

BAAL: A shameless bird! I'll have it. Act of rescue by desperate man! *He takes her by both arms and drags her into the thicket.*

Maple Trees in the Wind

Clouded sky. Baal and Ekart, sitting among the roots.

BAAL: Drink's needed, Ekart. Any money left?
EKART: No. Look at the maple in the wind!
BAAL: It's trembling.
EKART: Where's that girl you used to go around the bars with?
BAAL: Turn into a fish and look for her.
EKART: You overeat, Baal. You'll burst.
BAAL: I'd like to hear the bang.
EKART: Do you ever look into water when it's black and deep and got no fish in it? Don't ever fall in. Watch out for yourself. You're so very heavy, Baal.
BAAL: I'll watch out for somebody else. I've written a song. Do you want to hear it?
EKART: Read it, then I'll know you.
BAAL: It's called Death in the Forest.

And a man died deep in the primaeval woods
While the storm blew in torrents around him –
Died like an animal scrabbling for roots
Stared up through the trees, as the wind skimmed the woods
And the roar of the thunderclap drowned him.

Several of them stood to watch him go
And they strove to make his passage smoother
Telling him: We'll take you home now, brother.
But he forced them from him with a blow
Spat, and cried: and where's my home, d'you know?
That was home, and he had got no other.

Is your toothless mouth choking with pus?
How's the rest of you: can you still tell?
Must you die so slowly and with so much fuss?
We've just had your horse chopped into steaks for us.
Hurry up! They're waiting down in hell.

Then the forest roared above their head
And they watched him clasp a tree and stagger
And they heard his screams and what he said.
Each man felt an overwhelming dread
Clenched his fist or, trembling, drew his dagger:
So like them, and yet so nearly dead!

You're foul, useless, mad, you mangy bear!
You're a sore, a chancre, filthy creature!
Selfish beast, you're breathing up our air!
So they said. And he, the cancer there:
Let me live! Your sun was never sweeter!
– Ride off in the light without a care!

That's what none of them could understand:
How the horror numbed and made them shiver.
There's the earth holding his naked hand.
In the breeze from sea to sea lies land:
Here I lie in solitude for ever.

Yes, mere life, with its abundant weight
Pinned him so that even half-decayed
He pressed his dead body ever deeper.
At dawn he fell dead in the grassy shade.
Numb with shock, they buried him, and cold with hate
Covered him with undergrowth and creeper.

Then they rode in silence from that place
Turning round to see the tree again
Under which his body once had lain
Who felt dying was too sharp a pain:
The tree stood in the sun ablaze.
Each made the mark of the cross on his face
And rode off swiftly over the plain.

EKART: Well, well! I suppose it's come to that now.
BAAL: When I can't sleep at night I look up at the stars. It's just as good.

EKART: Is it?

BAAL *suspiciously:* But I don't do it often. It makes you weak.

EKART *after a pause:* You've made up a lot of poetry recently. You haven't had a woman for a long time, have you?

BAAL: Why?

EKART: I was thinking. Say no.

Baal gets up, stretches, looks at the top of the maple and laughs.

Inn

Evening. Ekart. The waitress. Watzmann. Johannes, in a shabby coat with a turned-up collar, hopelessly gone to seed. The waitress has the features of Sophie.

EKART: It's been eight years.

They drink. Wind.

JOHANNES: They say life only begins at twenty-five. That's when they get broader and have children.

Silence.

WATZMANN: His mother died yesterday. So he runs around trying to borrow money for the funeral. When he gets it he comes here. Then we can pay for the drinks. The landlord's a good man. He gives credit on a corpse which was a mother. *Drinks.*

JOHANNES: Baal! There's no wind left in his sails.

WATZMANN *to Ekart:* You must have to put up with a lot from him?

EKART: One can't spit in his face. The man's done for.

WATZMANN *to Johannes:* Does it distress you? Do you think about it?

JOHANNES: It's a waste of a man, I tell you. *Drinks.*

Silence.

WATZMANN: He's getting more and more disgusting.

EKART: Don't say that. I don't want to hear it. I love him. I don't resent him, because I love him. He's a child.

WATZMANN: He only does what he has to. Because he's so lazy.

EKART *goes to the door:* It's a mild night. The wind's warm. Like milk. I love all this. One should never drink. Or not so much. *Back to the table:* It's a mild night. Now and for another three weeks into the autumn a man can live on the road all right. *He sits down.*

WATZMANN: Do you want to leave tonight? You'd like to get rid of him, I suppose? He's a burden.

JOHANNES: You'd better be careful.

Baal enters slowly.

WATZMANN: Is that you, Baal?

EKART *hard:* What do you want now?

BAAL *enters, sits down:* What a miserable hole this place has turned into! *The waitress brings drink.*

WATZMANN: Nothing's changed here. Only you, it would appear, have got more refined.

BAAL: Is that still you, Luise?

Silence.

JOHANNES: Yes, it's agreeable here. – I have to drink, you see, drink a lot. It makes one strong. Even then one makes one's way to hell along a path of razors. But not in the same way. As if your legs were giving way under you, yielding, you know. So that you don't feel the razors at all. With springy loose joints. Besides, I never used to have ideas of this sort, really peculiar ones. Not while everything went well, when I lived a good bourgeois life. But now I have ideas, now that I've turned into a genius. Hm.

EKART *bursting out:* I'd like to be back in the forest, at dawn! The light between the trees is the colour of lemons! I want to go back up into the forest.

JOHANNES: That's something I don't understand, you must buy me another drink, Baal. It's really agreeable here.

BAAL: A gin for —

JOHANNES: No names! We know each other. I have such fearful dreams at night, you know, now and then. But only now and then. It really is agreeable here.

The wind. They drink.

WATZMANN *hums:*

The trees come in avalanches
Each very conveniently made.
You can hang yourself from their branches
Or loll underneath in their shade.

BAAL: Where was it like that? It was like that once.

JOHANNES: She's still afloat, you see. Nobody's found her. But sometimes I get a feeling she's being washed down my throat with all the drink, a very small corpse, half rotted. And she was already seventeen. Now there are rats and weed in her green hair, rather becoming . . . a little swollen and whitish, and filled with the stinking ooze from the river, completely black. She was always so clean. That's why she went into the river and began to stink.

WATZMANN: What is flesh? It decays just like the spirit. Gentlemen, I am completely drunk. Twice two is four. Therefore I am not drunk. But I have intimations of a higher world. Bow! . . . be hup! . . . humble! Put the old Adam aside! *Drinks heavily and shakily.* I've not reached rock bottom yet, not while I have my intimations, not while I can add up properly that twice two . . . What is this thing called two? Two – oo, curious word! Two! *Sits down.* *Baal reaches for his guitar and smashes the light with it.*

BAAL: Now I'll sing. *Sings:*

Sick from the sun, and eaten raw by the weather
A looted wreath crowning his tangled head
He called back the dreams of a childhood he had lost altogether
Forgot the roof, but never the sky overhead.

Then speaks: My voice is not entirely clear as a bell. *Tunes the guitar.*

EKART: Go on singing, Baal.

BAAL *goes on singing:*

O you whose life it has been always to suffer
You murderers they threw out from heaven and hell
Why did you not stay in the arms of your mother
Where it was quiet, and you slept, and all was well?

Speaks. The guitar's not in tune either.

WATZMANN: A good song. Very apt in my case. Romantic.

BAAL *goes on singing:*

Still he explores and scans the absinthe-green ocean
Though his mother give him up for lost
Grinning and cursing, or weeping at times with contrition
Always in search of that land where life is best.

WATZMANN: I can't find my glass. The table's rocking stupidly. Put the light on. How's a man to find his mouth?

EKART: Idiot! Can you see anything, Baal?

BAAL: No. I don't want to. It's good in the dark. With champagne in the blood and homesickness without memory. Are you my friend Ekart?

EKART *with an effort:* Yes, but sing!

BAAL *sings:*

Loafing through hells and flogged through paradises
Calm and grinning, with expressionless stare
Sometimes he dreams of a small field he recognizes
With blue sky overhead and nothing more.

JOHANNES: I'll always stay with you. You could take me with you. I hardly ever eat.

WATZMANN *has lit the lamp, with an effort:* Let there be light. Heh heh heh heh.

BAAL: It's blinding. *Gets up.*

Ekart, with the waitress on his lap, gets up with an effort and tries to take her arm from his neck.

EKART: What's the matter? This is nothing. It's ridiculous.

Baal gets ready to leap.

EKART: You're not jealous of her?

Baal gropes, a glass falls to the floor.

EKART: Why shouldn't I have women?

Baal looks at him.

EKART: Am I your lover?

Baal throws himself at him, chokes him.

The light goes out. Watzmann laughs drunkenly, the waitress screams. Other guests from the adjoining room enter with a lamp.

WATZMANN: He's got a knife.

THE WAITRESS: He's killing him. Oh God!

TWO MEN *hurl themselves on the wrestlers:* Blast you, man! Let go! – He's stabbed him! God Almighty!

Baal gets up. Sunset suddenly bursts into the room. The lamp goes out.

BAAL: Ekart!

10° E. of Greenwich

Forest. Baal with guitar, his hands in his pockets, walks off into the distance.

BAAL: The pale wind in the black trees! They're like Lupu's wet hair. At eleven the moon'll rise. It'll be light enough then. This is a small wood. I'll go where there are forests. I can move now that I'm on my own again. I must bear north. Follow the ribbed side of the leaves. I'll have to shrug off that little matter. Forward! *Sings:*

Baal will watch the vultures in the star-shot sky
Hovering patiently to see when Baal will die.

Disappearing.

Sometimes Baal shams dead. The vultures swoop.
Baal, without a word, will dine on vulture soup.

Gust of wind.

A Country Road

Evening. Wind. Rain. Two policemen struggle against the wind.

FIRST POLICEMAN: The black rain and this wailing wind! The bloody tramp!

SECOND POLICEMAN: It seems to me he keeps moving northwards towards the forests. It'll be impossible to find him there.

FIRST POLICEMAN: What is he?

SECOND POLICEMAN: Above all, a murderer. Before that, revue actor and poet. Then roundabout proprietor, woodsman, lover of a millionairess, convict and pimp. When he did the murder they caught him, but he's got the strength of an elephant. It was because of a waitress, a registered whore. He knifed his best and oldest friend because of her.

FIRST POLICEMAN: A man like that has no soul. He belongs to the beasts.

SECOND POLICEMAN: And he's childish too. He carries wood for old women, and nearly gets caught. He never had anything. Except for the waitress. That must have been why he killed his friend, another dubious character.

FIRST POLICEMAN: If only we could get some gin somewhere or a woman! Let's go! It's eerie. And there's something moving over there. *Both go.*

BAAL *comes out of the undergrowth with rucksack and guitar. He whistles through his teeth:* So he's dead? Poor little animal! Getting in my way. Now things are getting interesting. *He follows the men.*

Wind.

Hut in the Forest

Night. Wind. Baal on a dirty bed. Men at cards and drink.

A MAN *by Baal:* What do you want? You're at your last gasp. A child could see that. And who's going to look after you? Have you got anyone? That's it! That's it! Grit your teeth! Got any teeth left? Now and then it even gets the ones that could go on enjoying themselves, millionaires! But you don't even have any papers. Don't you be afraid, the world'll keep rolling, round as a ball, tomorrow morning the wind'll whistle. See the situation in a more reasonable light. Tell yourself it's a rat that's on the way out. That's it! Don't move! You've no teeth left.

THE MEN: Is it still pissing? We'll have to spend the night with the corpse. – Shut your mouth! Trumped! – Got any breath left, fatty? Sing us a song! 'Baal grew up within the . . .' – Let him be! He'll be a cold man before the black rain's stopped. On with the game! – He drank like a sieve but there's something about that pale hunk that makes you think about yourself. That's something he didn't have crooned over his cradle. – Ten of clubs! Keep your cards up, please! That's no way to play; if you're not going to be serious, you can't get a good game going.

Silence, except for a few curses.

BAAL: What's the time?

ONE OF THE MEN: Eleven. Are you going?

BAAL: Soon. Are the roads bad?

THE MAN: Rain.

THE MEN *getting up:* It's stopped raining. Time to go. – Everything'll be soaking wet. – Another excuse for him to do nothing.

They pick up the axes.

A MAN *stops in front of Baal and spits:* Good night and goodbye. Have you had it?

ANOTHER MAN: Are you on the way out? Incognito?

A THIRD MAN: Arrange your smelly periods better tomorrow, if you don't mind. We'll be working till twelve and then we want to eat.

BAAL: Can't you stay a little longer?

ALL *amid loud laughter:* Do you want us to play mother? – Do you want to sing us your swan song? – Do you want to confess, you old soak? – Can't you throw up on your own?

BAAL: If you could stay half an hour.

ALL *amid loud laughter:* You know what? Snuff out on your own! – Let's get moving! The wind's died down. – What's the matter?

THE MAN: I'll follow.

BAAL: It can't last much longer, gentlemen. *Laughter.* You won't like dying on your own, gentlemen! *Laughter.*

ANOTHER MAN: Old woman! Here's a souvenir! *Spits in his face.*

They go.

BAAL: Twenty minutes.

The men leave by the open door.

THE MAN *in the door:* Stars.

BAAL: Wipe the spit away!

THE MAN *to him:* Where?

BAAL: On my forehead.

THE MAN: Done! What are you laughing at?

BAAL: I like the taste.

THE MAN *indignant:* You're done for. Good-bye! *With his axe to the door.*

BAAL: Thanks.

THE MAN: Is there anything else . . . but I have to go to work. Jesus. Corpses!

BAAL: You! Come closer! *The man bends down.* It was very beautiful . . .

THE MAN: What was, you crazy hen? I nearly said capon.

BAAL: Everything.

THE MAN: Snob! *Laughs loudly, goes, the door remains open, one sees the blue night.*

BAAL *uneasy:* You! You there!

THE MAN *at the window:* Mmmm?
BAAL: Are you going?
THE MAN: To work.
BAAL: Where?
THE MAN: What's that got to do with you?
BAAL: What's the time?
THE MAN: A quarter past eleven. *Goes.*
BAAL: He's gone.
Silence.
Mother! Tell Ekart to go away, the sky's so damned near too, you can touch it, everything's soaking wet again. Sleep. One. Two. Three. Four. It's suffocating in here. It must be light outside. I want to go out. *Raises himself.* I will go out. Dear Baal. *Sharply.* I'm not a rat. It must be light outside. Dear Baal. You can get to the door. You've still got knees, it's better in the door. Damn it! Dear Baal! *He crawls on all fours to the threshold.* Stars . . . mmm. *He crawls out.*

Early Morning in the Forest

Woodcutters.

A WOODCUTTER: Give me the bottle! Listen to the birds!
ANOTHER: It'll be a hot day.
A THIRD: There's plenty of trees left standing that'll have to be down before nightfall.
A FOURTH: He'll be cold by now.
THE THIRD: Yes. Yes. He'll be cold by now.
THE SECOND: Yes. Yes.
THE THIRD: We could have had the eggs now if he hadn't eaten them all. There's a man for you, stealing eggs on his deathbed. First he kept moaning at me, I got sick of that. He never got a whiff of the bottle in all three days, thank God. It's inconsiderate. Eggs in a corpse.
THE FIRST: He had a way of laying himself down in the dirt,

and then he never got up again, and he knew it. It was like a ready-made bed to him. He lay down carefully. Did anybody know him? What's his name? What did he do?

THE FOURTH: We'll have to bury him, anyway. Give me the bottle!

THE THIRD: I asked him, as the death-rattle was in his throat, what are you thinking about? I always want to know what goes on in a man's head then. I'm still listening to the rain, he said. I went cold all over. I'm still listening to the rain, he said.

Notes and Variants

Texts by Brecht

PROLOGUE TO THE 1918 VERSION

The subject of this play is the very ordinary story of a man who sings a hymn to summer in a grog-shop without selecting his audience – together with the consequences of summer, grog and song. The man is not a particularly modern poet. Baal has not been handicapped by Nature. He belongs to the period of the play's performance. Remember Socrates and Verlaine, with their lamentable skulls. For actors (who love extremes, except when they can get away with mediocrities), Baal is neither a specially comic character nor a specially tragic one. Like all wild animals he is serious. As for the play, the author has managed to find a message in it: it sets out to prove that you can have your cake if you are prepared to pay for it. And even if you aren't. So long as you pay . . . The play is the story neither of a single incident nor of many, but of a life. Originally it was called *Baal eats! Baal dances!! Baal is transfigured!!!*

[GW *Schriften zum Theater*, p. 954.]

PROLOGUE TO THE 1926 VERSION

This dramatic biography shows the life story of the man Baal as it took place in the first part of this century. You see before you Baal the abnormality trying to come to terms with the twentieth-century world. Baal the relative man, Baal the passive genius, the whole phenomenon of Baal from his first appearance among civilized beings up to his horrific end, with his unprecedented consumption of ladies of high degree, in his dealings with his fellow-humans. This creature's life was one of sensational immorality. In the stage version it has been considerably toned down. The performance begins with Baal's first appearance as a poet among civilized beings in the year 1904. As a preliminary you will see Baal in the round from several aspects and hear his version of how he used to perform his famous Hymn of Baal the Great, accompanied on his own unique invention, the tin-stringed banjo.

[Ibid., pp. 954–5.]

THE MODEL FOR BAAL

The dramatic biography called *Baal* treats of the life of a man who really existed. This was a certain Josef K., whom I heard about from people who retained clear memories of the man's person and the commotion created by his activities. K. was the illegitimate son of a washerwoman. He soon made a bad name for himself. Though without formal education of any sort he is said to have been able to impress the most highly educated people by his extraordinarily well-informed talk. A friend told me that the idiosyncrasy of his movements (when taking a cigarette, when seating himself on a chair, and so on) made such a mark on a number of (mainly) young people that they wanted to imitate him. His carefree way of life, however, led him to sink ever deeper, particularly since he never started anything himself but shamelessly took advantage of every opportunity offered him. A number of shady episodes were laid at his door, including a girl's suicide. He was a trained mechanic, though so far as we know he never worked. When A. became too hot for him he went off on protracted wanderings with a broken-down medical student, returning to A. in about 1911. There his friend was killed in an affray with knives in a grog-shop on the Lauterlech, almost certainly by K. himself. At all events he then disappeared with remarkable suddenness from A., and is supposed to have died miserably in the Black Forest.

['Das Urbild Baals', from *Die Szene*, Berlin, January 1926, reprinted in GW *Schriften zum Theater*, p. 955. Elisabeth Hauptmann's 'Notizen über Brechts Arbeit 1926' on p. 241 of the *Sinn und Form* special Brecht issue of 1957 cites her diary for 18 January: 'Wrote the "Model" for Baal for *Die Szene* in the form of a newspaper report. The model for Baal, the "anti-social" man, is an Augsburg mechanic.' This has not prevented commentators from taking at their face value both the report and Brecht's claim to have written it.]

BAD BAAL THE ANTI-SOCIAL MAN

but that is what makes bad baal the antisocial man great
that the report of his enemy
describing him with my voice is
permeated by his
accusing me that i
a delighted onlooker
while he was exploiting the exploiters
and making use of the users
started treating him more harshly
as soon as he derided my own rules
but that is his offence
and why he is called antisocial
because in making trivial demands of him
the perfect state would appear like an exploiter.

['Baal', from Dieter Schmidt (ed.): *Baal. Der böse Baal der asoziale*, Suhrkamp, 1968, p. 90. This poem, which is not included in GW, is part of the material relating to the Baal *Lehrstücke* project discussed on pp. 68–69 below.]

ON LOOKING THROUGH MY FIRST PLAYS (ii)

Baal is a play which could present all kinds of difficulties to those who have not learnt to think dialectically. No doubt they will see it as a glorification of unrelieved egotism and nothing more. Yet here is an individual standing out against the demands and discouragements of a world whose form of production is designed for exploitation rather than usefulness. We cannot tell how Baal would react to having his talents employed; what he is resisting is their misuse. Baal's art of life is subject to the same fate as any other art under capitalism: it is attacked. He is anti-social, but in an anti-social society.

Twenty years after completing *Baal* I was preoccupied with an idea (for an opera) related to the same basic theme. There is a carved wooden Chinese figure, two or three inches high and sold in thousands, representing the fat little god of happiness, contentedly stretching himself. This god was to arrive from the East after a great war and enter the devastated cities, trying to persuade people to fight for their personal happiness and well-being. He acquires followers of various sorts, and becomes subject to persecution by the authorities when some of them start proclaiming that the peasants ought to be given land, the workers to take over the factories, and the workers' and peasants' children to seize the schools. He is arrested and condemned to death. And now the executioners practise their arts on the little god of happiness. But when they hand him poison he just smacks his lips; when they cut his head off he at once grows a new one; when they hang him from the gallows he starts an irresistibly lively dance, etc., etc. *Humanity's urge for happiness can never be entirely killed.*

For the present edition of *Baal* the original version of the first and last scenes has been restored. Otherwise I have left the play as it was, not having the strength to alter it. I admit (and advise you): this play is lacking in wisdom.

['Bei Durchsicht meiner ersten Stücke.' Foreword to *Stücke I*, all editions but the first. GW *Schriften zum Theater*, pp. 947–8. For a more accurate view of the revisions to the first and last scenes, see p. 68 below.]

Editorial Note

For the following note and for the writings by Brecht quoted in it the editors have drawn gratefully and extensively on the two volumes of 'materials' edited by Dieter Schmidt, *Baal. Drei Fassungen* and *Baal. Der böse Baal der asoziale. Texten, Varianten und Materialien*, published by Suhrkamp-Verlag in 1966 and 1968 respectively ('edition suhrkamp' numbers 170 and 248).

Brecht's first play was not written in four days and for a bet, as has been alleged, but developed from a paper which he read in the spring of 1918 to Professor Artur Kutscher's theatre seminar at Munich University. His subject was Hanns Johst, the Expressionist novelist and playwright who later wrote the Nazi play *Schlageter* and at the end of 1933 became president of the (purged) Prussian Academy. Brecht undertook to write a 'counter-play' to Johst's *Der Einsame* (The Lonely One), an emotionalized account of the life of the nineteenth-century dramatist Christoph Dietrich Grabbe, which the Munich Kammerspiele were presenting. A first draft was complete by mid-May, and a month later he could write to his lifelong friend Caspar Neher:

> My play:
>
> Baal eats! Baal dances!! Baal is transfigured!!!
>
> What's Baal up to?
>
> 24 scenes
>
> is ready and typed – a substantial tome. I hope to get somewhere with it.

He revised the play in the spring of 1919, after his military service and the writing of the earliest draft of *Drums in the Night*. That was the version first submitted to publishers and theatre managements, but Brecht appears to have decided that it was too long – there were 29 scenes – and too wild, and before its publication he overhauled it yet a third time, jettisoning about one-third of the 1919 text. Publication should have taken place some time in the second half of 1920, but the original publishers were by then already in trouble with the censorship over other books, and only a few copies for Brecht's own use were ever printed. The rights were transferred to another firm (Kiepenheuer of Potsdam) who brought the book out two years later at the time of the première of *Drums in the Night*, virtually unchanged apart from the addition of the first woodcutters' scene.

This first published version was the play as we now have it, apart from the first and last scenes. It was republished in 1953 as the first volume of Brecht's collected *Stücke*; then in 1955 scene 1 was given its present form (including the two poems quoted from the Munich Expressionist periodical *Revolution*, which are in fact Georg Heym's 'Der Baum' and 'Vorbereitung' by the then East German Minister of Culture, Johannes R. Becher), while Brecht restored the final scene which he deleted from the proofs in 1920. What Brecht says in his own note of 1954 is not precisely right, since neither of these scenes is in its original form. But clearly he was content to leave it as an early work.

In the later 1920s he felt otherwise. The version which he himself staged at the Deutsches Theater in February 1926 (a single afternoon performance by the 'Junge Bühne' – and *Baal's* only performance in Berlin to this day) was a largely new, much shorter play called *Life Story of the Man Baal*. As will be seen below, it retained only eleven of the published scenes, which were altered so as to set Baal in the emergent technological society of the first decade of the century. They were stripped of much of their original lyricism and given an 'epic' framework by means of titles to each scene. Brecht wanted this version to appear as an appendix to the *Stücke* edition of the 1950s, but it remained unpublished till 1966. Its only other known performances were in Vienna in 1926 (with a prologue by Hofmannsthal) and in Kassel the year after.

Around 1930 – the dates and also the intended arrangement of the fragmentary typescript are uncertain – he planned a number of linked *Lehrstücke* (or didactic playlets) about the character he now called *Bad Baal the Antisocial Man*. Here he thought of making Baal appear in various guises –

> guest/whore/judge/dealer (bulls)/engineer (only concerned with experiment)/suppliant – in need of help (exploiting other people's wish to be exploited)/nature-lover/demagogue/worker (strikebreaker)/mother/historian/soldier/lover (baker's apprentice scene from 'breadshop')/as parson/as civil servant/the 2 coats

– but apart from a reception where Baal is guest and the Baal Hymn is sung this plan has very little to do with the play. The writing is deadpan, with strange word order and virtually no punctuation apart from full stops. Brecht's aphoristic *alter ego* Herr Keuner appears, and the only *Baal* character apart from Baal himself is Lupu. Some idea of the style can be got from the beginning of 'Bad Baal the Antisocial Man and the Two Coats', which is one of the few complete episodes:

> BAAL: all night i have been going in increasing cold through the forests towards where they get darker. the evening was icy. the night was icier and a crowd of stars crept into a whiteish fog towards morning. today the bushes occupy the least space of the entire year. whatever is soft freezes. whatever is hard breaks.
>
> THE LEFT-HAND CHORUS the best thing is
> the cold comes before the warmth
> everything makes itself as small
> as it can. everything is
> so sparingly silent only
> thinking becomes im-
> practicable and then
> comes the warmth
>
> THE POOR MAN it is cold. i have no coat. i'm freezing. perhaps that grand gentleman can tell me what i can do against the cold. good day sir . . .

In 1938 Brecht again looked at the play with a view to the Malik-Verlag collected edition of his work (which was never completed). 'A pity,' he then noted: 'it was always a torso, and on top of that it underwent a number of operations . . . Its meaning almost disappeared. Baal the provocateur, the admirer of things as they are, who believes in living life to the full, other people's lives as well as his own. His "do what amuses you" could be very rewarding if properly handled. Wonder if I could find the time'. That is, aside from the *Lehrstücke* plan, which was still on the agenda. A few months later he seems to have written that off to judge from a diary note of 4 March 1939:

> Today I finally realized why I never managed to turn out those little *Lehrstücke* about the adventures of 'Bad Baal the Antisocial Man'. Antisocial people aren't important. The really antisocial people are the owners of the means of production and other sources of life, and they are only antisocial as such. There are also their helpers and their helpers' helpers, of course, but again

> only as such. It is *the* gospel of humanity's enemies that there are such things as antisocial instincts, antisocial personalities and so on.

He also came to feel that he had made a mistake in seeing socialism as a matter of social order rather than of productivity, which may have been another reason underlying his more sympathetic judgement of Baal at the end of his life.

THE VERSIONS OF 1918, 1919 AND 1920–2 (*first published version*)

Numbers in square brackets refer to the scene order of the final text. Other numbers to that of the particular script under discussion

Though *Baal* at first appears to have little structure, so that Brecht could change scenes around, or add or delete them, without greatly affecting the play's character, there are nine basic scenes which recur in the same order in every version, together with four others* which are in all except the 1926 text. They are: [1] (the opening party scene), [2] (Baal and Johannes), [3] (the first tavern scene), [4 i] (Baal and Johanna, after the seduction), [4 iii] (first scene with Sophie), [6]* (second ditto), [7] (cabaret scene), [8]* (Baal and Ekart), [15] (Baal reading a poem to Ekart, who speaks of his girl), [17]* (Baal reads 'Death in the Forest'). [18] (last tavern scene, with the murder of Ekart), [20]* (the two gendarmes), and [21] (the death scene in the forest hut). Accordingly, we shall start by describing the more significant changes in these scenes, from one version to another up to 1922.

[1] In the first two versions it is a grand party: full evening dress. The host and other guests are not named; the host's wife is not mentioned. Unspecified poems by Stramm and Novotny (whoever *he* was) are read; Baal, who is a clerk in the host's office, calls them drivel. The servants try to throw him out, but he fights them off, saying, 'I'll show you who's master.'

The 1922 version is virtually the same as the final text, less the character of Pschierer and all between the first remark of the Young Man and the last remark of the Young Woman. The scene ends, after Piller's last jibe, with Johannes asking Baal if he may visit him and Emilie saying, 'I'm sorry for him.'

[2] Baal's speeches are longer than in the final version, but the scene is not essentially changed.

[3] In 1918 it is a bourgeois bar. Baal reads the 'Ballad of Evelyn Roe' (now in Brecht's collected poems), is applauded and introduces Johannes and 'Mr Ekart, a brilliant composer who is passing through'. He insults the bourgeois, who fail to pay for his drinks; he refuses to join Ekart on his wanderings because Marie the waitress, who is in love with him, cannot come too. Johannes leads him away.

In 1919 this becomes the Inn with an audience of drivers to whom he sings 'Orge's song'. Johannes brings Johanna; Emmi arrives, identified by Baal as 'wife of my office boss' and described as *well-dressed, nervous, rather domineering.* It is virtually the final version.

[4 i] Essentially the final version, though in 1918 Johanna is called Anna. Instead of asking Baal if he still loves her, she asks, 'Do you love me?' *in a small voice, breathlessly.*

[4 iii] Sophie Dechant in 1918 appears dressed in white. She is an actress, on her way to play (presumably Hebbel's) Judith. Much of the final version is there – Baal calling her a white cloud, her reference to Baal's ugliness, her virginity, her declaration that she loves him – till Baal's mother comes in, accusing him of having whores in his room. He says Sophie is to be his wife, and asks her if she will. A piano is playing all the time, off.

In 1919 the scene has been largely rewritten. Sophie ceases to be an actress and takes her eventual form. Baal still says she is to be his wife, but no longer asks her.

By 1922 the mother is cut out of the play. Baal's long opening speech, which originally introduced another scene with his mother (see below) is added to this one. Johannes makes his brief appearance. Sophie's name is changed to Barger, and there is no mention of her becoming Baal's wife. Instead of the piano there is intermittently the beggar's hurdy-gurdy playing *Tristan.*

[6] In 1918 it is 'Night', with no place given. Sophie says they are penniless, and wants to go back to the stage. Baal says he will go on the stage: in a cabaret. He sings the verse which later introduces 4 (ii).

In 1919 the scene is rewritten. It is a bedroom in the summer, and several phrases of the dialogue survive into the final version. It is now Baal who says, 'Do you realize we've got no money?' The cabaret is not mentioned.

In 1922 there is no song, and the scene is set out of doors in May, as we have it.

[7] In 1918 there is an unnamed compère instead of Mjurk. There is no Lupu and no mention of the agreement about schnaps. The dialogue is differently phrased, but the only major differences from the ultimate version are: (1) the irruption of a group of Young Artists, who tell Baal: 'Your latest poem in the *Phoebus* is good, but too affectedly simple – Princess Ebing's taking an interest in you. She's hot stuff. Lucky fellow!'; (2) the song which Baal sings, dressed in tails and a child's sailor hat, which goes roughly:

If a woman's hips are ample
Then I want her in the hay
Skirt and stockings all a-rumple
(cheerfully) – for that's my way.

If the woman bites in pleasure
Then I wipe it clean with hay
My mouth and her lap together
(thoroughly) – for that's my way.

If the woman goes on loving
When I feel too tired to play
I just smile and go off waving
(amiably) – for that's my way.

The 1919 version is textually the same, except for the replacement of 'Compère' by 'Nigger John' throughout. For Nigger John, see below.

In 1922 Mjurk, Lupu, and the final song make their appearance. There is a typescript of the song dated 21 January 1920.

[8] Basically the same in all versions.

[15] 1918 and 1919 (slightly lengthened) versions show Ekart talking about his pale-faced girl as an experience of the past; Baal goes to sleep while he is talking about her. The poem which Baal recites to him is not the 'Drowned Girl' (as in the 1922 text) but 'The Song of the Cloud in the Night' (in the collected poems).

[17] In 1918 the scene is set outside a country tavern. The text is almost word for word the same as in the final version, apart from some slight variations in the poem 'Death in the Forest', until what is now the end of the scene. Thereupon Baal says 'I'll go and get one' (i.e., a woman), and breaks into the dance which has started inside the tavern. There is almost a fight with the man whose

partner Baal pulls away from him, then Baal suddenly crumples and leaves.

In 1919 the setting becomes 'Maple Trees in the Wind', and the dance episode is detached to make a separate short scene, which Brecht dropped in the third version.

[18] The 1918 and 1919 versions are almost identical apart from the absence of Johannes from the former and certain differences in the arrangement of the verses. Baal here arrives, on the top of his form, having sold a book of his poems to a publisher. 'I want meat! What's your name, kids, and what's your price? I'm as choosy as a vicar. But watch what I can do. I'll pay for everything!' He orders champagne (in the final version there is an allusion to this left after the third verse of the Ballad) and, with Luise on his knee (who does not yet look like Sophie) sings an obscene, blasphemous, and largely untranslatable song about the Virgin. Watzmann, whose character was even then unexplained, sings in lieu of 'The trees come in avalanches':

When the hatred and venom he's swallowed
Are more than his gullet can take
He may well draw a knife from his pocket
And languidly sever his neck.

At the end of the scene, before Baal attacks Ekart, Ekart tries to get Luise off his lap, saying, 'Oh, rubbish! Gentlemen! Let's drink to fair shares between brothers!'

There is a draft of January 1920 showing the waitress with Sophie's features and Baal a wreck, as in the 1922 text, which also substitutes the new dialogue between Baal and Ekart at the end.

[20] The dialogue between the two policemen is little changed. In 1918 and 1919 three other professions are attributed to Baal: gardener, city clerk, and journalist. Those of roundabout proprietor, woodcutter, and millionairess's lover only appear in the 1922 version.

[22] This scene has remained essentially unchanged from the 1918 version, apart from Baal's last speech, which both there and in 1919 runs:

> Dear God. Gone. *Groans.* It's not so simple. My God, it's not so simple. If only I. One. Two. Three. Four. Five. Six. Not much help. Dear God. *Dear* God. *Feverishly:* Mother! Send Ekart away! Oh, Mary! The sky's so damned near. Almost touch it. My heart's thumping. One. Two. Three. Four.

Whimpers, then all of a sudden, loudly: I can't. I won't. It's stifling here. *Quite distinctly:* It must be clear outside. I want to. *Raising himself with difficulty.* Baal, I want to go out. *Sharply:* I'm not a rat. *He tumbles off the bed, and falls.* Hell. Dear God! As far as the door! *He crawls to the threshold.* Stars ... hm. *He crawls out.*

In the 1922 version the five invocations of God and one of Mary are replaced by the three invocations of 'Dear Baal'.

Other scenes:—

Seven further scenes were cut or telescoped with others when Brecht revised the play in 1919. Two of these represent a loss to the narrative: 9, which shows Baal arrested on Corpus Christi day because he is drunkenly outraged by the cutting of branches for the procession, and scene 11, where a theatre review which he has written is rejected by the manager of his newspaper, and the editor then sacks him. The main points of the other five scenes (which elaborate the affairs with Emmy and Johanna, show him being visited in prison by his mother, and later forcing an unnamed girl to sell herself for him) are incorporated in or anticipated by other changes.

There are three new long scenes in the 1919 revision, and five others of which two appear in this version only. The long ones are [10] the scene over the body of the dead woodcutter Teddy, [13] the Bolleboll–Gougou scene, and [9] Baal's pretence of buying bulls. The two scenes subsequently cut are scene 8, immediately following the first Sophie scene, where the barman Nigger John offers Baal (in a top hat) a job in his cabaret; and scene 19, preceding the 'Death in the Forest' scene, where Baal, Ekart and a new girl called Anna try to get a night's lodging. A man opens his window and says that Anna can come in his room and the others sleep in the hay.

ANNA: I'm so frightened. I don't want to be alone.
BAAL: You won't be alone.

The man says he can offer them soup with milk and fresh bread. 'The young lady gets the cream, hahaha.'

ANNA: I must do whatever you want, but I'm sure it's not right.

BAAL: Nonsense. Warmth is right and soup is right. Get on in! You've been a burden so far; now you can make yourself useful.

The other new scenes are [12], where Baal and Ekart abandon the pregnant Sophie; an early version of [11], with Baal and Ekart in a hut in the winter; and the very short [14], in the undergrowth by the river, where Baal says, 'I don't care for women any longer . . .'

In the 1922 text the position of all these new scenes is changed relatively to the basic framework. Four more are added, of which [4 ii], where the two sisters visit Baal's room, is the most substantial. [5] with the drunk tramp restores the point of one of the scenes cut in 1919. [16] is the scene with Ekart's pale red-haired girl, now very much part of the present. [19] is Baal's brief passage across the stage '10° East of Greenwich'. Nine scenes are cut, including the two 1919 additions mentioned above and the detached (quarrel at the dance) episode of [17]. The others are two scenes with Baal's mother, who is thus eliminated from the play (one, originally scene 4, showing her reprimanding her son for his drunkenness, the other preceding the last tavern scene and showing her on her deathbed); a scene following the cabaret episode, with Baal arrested by the police in a café; and the next scene after that, with Baal in prison being reasoned with by a clergyman:

CLERGYMAN: You're sinking deeper all the time.

BAAL: Thanks to my immense weight. But I enjoy it. I'm going down. Aren't I? But I'm doing all right, aren't I? Am I going off course? Am I a coward? Am I trying to stave off the consequences? Am I scared of you? Death and I are friends. Hardship's my whore. I'm humbler than you.

CLERGYMAN: You're too light to go under. You cheerful bankrupt.

BAAL: Sometimes I'm like a diver whose cables and breathing tubes have been cut, going for a walk all alone in the depths.

CLERGYMAN: Nothing is so terrible as loneliness. Nobody is alone with us. We are all brothers.

BAAL: Being alone has so far been my strength. I don't want a second man in my skin . . .

Finally, two snort scenes are deleted near the end of the play: one with a moralizing Baal interrupting lovers on a park bench, the other between [20] and [21], where Baal, on the run at night, tries vainly to get a peasant girl to walk with him.

'LIFE STORY OF THE MAN BAAL' (1926)

This later typescript is published in the second of Dieter Schmidt's volumes, and is subtitled 'Dramatic Biography by Bertolt Brecht. (Stage adaptation of "Baal".)' It consists of the nine basic scenes in shortened and largely rewritten form, plus [12] and [19], and a new short scene only found in this version (scene 9 below). All except scene 1 are given titles. Some of the names are spelt differently. The play begins with seven verses of the Hymn (verses 1, 2, 4, and the last four) sung by Baal, who then leaves the stage.

Scene 1. Room with dining table.

Enter Mäch, Emilie Mäch, Johannes Schmidt, Dr Piller, Baal.

MÄCH *while Baal stands eating at the buffet:* I think I may claim to have been the first to foresee your path to those heights of fame for which born geniuses are predestined. Genius has always suffered persecution; as it listens in its unworldly way to higher voices it is brought down to the cold realities of the world. I would like to think that my salon had been the first to welcome you, before the distinction of the Kleist Prize snatches you away from us. Will you have a glass of wine? . . .

Johannes says that Baal sings his poems to the taxi-drivers.

MÄCH: Fantastic.

EMILIE:

With cynical penury of airy poems
Of an orange-flavoured bitterness
Chilled on ice, black Malayan
Hair over the eyes! O opium smoke! . . .
Is that really by you?

JOHANNES: That's Herr Baal's. They generally give him three glasses of kirsch for each song. And one glass for a look at the special instrument he invented, which he says posterity will know as Baal's original tin-stringed banjo.

MÄCH: Fantastic.

JOHANNES: It's in a café at a goods station.

EMILIE: I suppose you've read a great deal?

MÄCH: Just let him eat in peace for the moment. Let him recover. Art's hard work too, you know. Help yourself to brandy, Hennessy, it's all there.

EMILIE: You live in a garage?
BAAL: 64a Holzstrasse.
MÄCH: Fantastic. Weren't you a mechanic?
EMILIE:

> In wind-crazed huts of light paper
> O you bitterness and gaiety of the world
> When the moon, that soft white animal
> Falls out of colder skies.

Apart from one remark of Baal's, who announces: 'In the year 1904 Joseph Mäch gives Baal a light for his cigar,' the last two-thirds of the scene are close to our version from after the last remark of the Young Lady (on p. 8) to the end. Then the Servant is cut (as in 1922) and, after Johannes has asked if he may visit Baal, Emilie says: 'I don't know. I like him. He needs looking after.' Then a new closing speech from Baal:

> It's raining. At the time of the Flood they all went into the ark. All the animals, by agreement. The only time the creatures of this world have ever agreed about anything. They really all did come. But the ichthyosaurus didn't. Everybody said he should get on board, but he was very busy just then. Noah himself warned him the Flood was coming. But he quietly said, 'I don't believe it'. He was universally unpopular when he drowned. Ah yes, they all said, the ichthyosaurus won't be coming. He was the oldest beast of them all, well qualified by his great experience to say whether such a thing as a Flood was or was not feasible. It's very possible that if a similar situation ever arises I shan't get on board either.

Baal's Unhesitating Abuse of Divine Gifts.

Scene 2. Garage.

The tone is drier, but essentially the scene is a condensed version of the Baal–Johannes scene as we have it, except that it ends with Baal saying not 'you should avoid it' but 'I think you should bring her to me'.

Baal Abuses his Power over a Woman.

Scene 3. 'Pub.'

Baal, Eckart, a tart. Taxi-drivers at the bar.

ECKART: I'm on the move. I've had just about enough of this town. Last night I slept with this lady and realized that I'm too grown up for that sort of thing. My advice is to hang all ovaries on the hook once and for all. I'm for freedom of movement till one's forty-five. Plato says the same if I'm not mistaken.
BAAL: Where are you going?
ECKART: The South of France, I think. Apart from anything else they seem to have a different type of town there. The plan is different, to start with, because there's enough light and that guarantees order. Are you coming?
BAAL: Got any money?
ECKART: Up to a point.
BAAL: Enough for a train?
ECKART: Enough for feet.
BAAL: When are you off?
ECKART: Today. I'm leaving this pub at eleven-thirty.
BAAL: How come?
ECKART: I've got a photo of Marseilles. Three dingy ellipses. Are you coming?
BAAL: Possibly. I don't know yet.

A version of the scene as we have it then begins, with Baal's account of Mäch's party and then Johannes's entrance. Johanna, however, is now fifteen: two years younger. It is not specified what ballad Baal sings. Eckart having already made his appeal does not make it again, but before singing Baal says:

Today, my friends, I was made an offer which no doubt has erotic motives. Kirsch, Luise. The man in question is about to move off. He's just smoking his last cigar and drinking his last kirsch. I'm probably going to say 'not yet'. Drink up, Emilie. Obviously I'm in the market for counter-offers. I imagine that poses a problem for you, Emilie.
EMILIE: I don't know what's the matter with you today . . .

After the driver Horgauer has kissed Emilie the ending is wholly changed. The taxi-drivers applaud and Johanna tells Baal he should be ashamed of himself, as in our version. Then Emilie tells Johanna:

> Don't pay any attention to me. I've been criticized for not having enough temperament for this kind of place. But perhaps I've shown that my dirtiness has been underestimated.

ECKART: Bill!

BAAL: Emmi, you haven't paid. You can relax. It's over now. Forget it.

ECKART: I'm going.

BAAL: Where?

ECKART: South of France. Are you coming too?

BAAL: Can't you put it off?

ECKART: No, I don't want to do that. Are you coming or not?

BAAL: No.

64a Holzstrasse

Scene 4. Garage.

A condensed conflation of scenes [4 i] and [4 ii]. The tone of Baal's dialogue with Johanna is drier. She has no remorse, and is only concerned about getting dressed. The Porter's Wife irrupts after Baal's 'Give me a kiss', and berates him in much the same shocked words as the landlady of [4 ii]. Then back to the finish of [4 i], with Baal saying:

> Off home with you! Tell Johnny Schmidt we just came in for five minutes because it was raining.

JOHANNA: Tell Johnny Schmidt it was raining. *Exit.*

BAAL: Johanna! There she goes.

– and no music.

Two Years later: Baal Discovers a (to him) New Kind of Love

Scene 5. Garage.

On the wall a nude drawing of a woman. Baal arrives with Miss Barger.

BAAL: My workshop.

BARGER: Excuse me, but I'm going back down.

BAAL: You can't just do that.

BARGER: They'll find me here. There was a man who followed us when you came up and spoke to me outside.

BAAL: Nobody'll find you here.

BARGER: Out there you told me you were a photographer.

BAAL: That's what I said out there, wasn't it?

BARGER: Then I'm going.

BAAL: There was something particular I wanted to ask you.

BARGER: No.

BAAL: What are you scared of all of a sudden?

BARGER: I'm not the least bit scared.

BAAL: Oh. That's a drawing I did to help make matters clear. If you don't like it we'll take it down. But you see, I know you inside and out; there's no mystery. There! *He scratches out the drawing with his knife.*

BARGER: Holy mother of God! *Screams.*

BAAL: What are you screaming about? Don't make such a noise. They'll hear you next door. Is it the knife? *Picks up a bottle.* Nothing left in there. No air left either. As for the meat! The meat's pathetic. It's not meat at all, just skin and a couple of fibres. I don't call that meat. Altogether this planet's a washout. A piece of impertinence. All fixed up for visitors. With mountains. But there aren't any mountains. That's what the valleys are for. Stuff the one into the other and the stupid planet's flat again. There, now you've stopped.

BARGER: Shall I stay with you?

BAAL: What?

BARGER: Your drawing's very ugly. But you look discontented. Me too. When I was fourteen the butcher next door wouldn't even let me sweep the snow off his pavement because I was too ugly. Lately men have taken to turning round and looking at me in the street; what I've got won't last long; I think I ought to make use of it. I don't think it has to be a man in a smart hat. But it's no good having something that isn't made use of.

BAAL: Now could that surprising way of talking be because she's scared of death?

BARGER: Scared of death? Have you had ideas of that sort?

BAAL: Don't get up. You don't suit. *Smokes.* Get your voice in operation again. It was a great moment. I'm abandoning hope. Seven years in this room, eighteen months' conscious abstention from food, washing out my mind with unadulterated consumption of alcohol. Never in my life having done the least little thing, I'm on the verge of entering new territory. This place of mine is all worn out. Mostly by systematic overestimation of everything, I suppose. I can see them saying that at the time of my death table and wall had been utterly worn away. And I still have to resolve the permanent problem of my life: the devising of an evil deed.

BARGER: It isn't easy, but I'm sure I can understand you if I really try.

BAAL: I give up. You talk now. Nobody shall say I neglected anything. You've got a woman's face. In your case one could perhaps cause seven pounds of disaster, where with most women one can't even cause two. How old are you?

BARGER: Twenty-four in June.

BAAL: How many men have you had in your life?

Barger says nothing.

BAAL: Then you've got that behind you. Any relatives?

BARGER: Yes, a mother.

BAAL: Is she old?

BARGER: She's sixty.

BAAL: Then she's got used to evil.

BARGER: They oughtn't to blame me. I can't support myself.

BAAL: You'll learn.

BARGER: You're asking an awful lot. You're so ugly it's terrifying. What's your name?

BAAL: Baal.

Baal Earns Money for the Last Time.

Scene 6. The Prickly Pear nightclub.

This is scene [7], still the 'Small, swinish café', with the difference that the parts of the Soubrette and her accompanist have been considerably written up, that the text of Baal's song is not given, and that when Baal escapes through the lavatory window it is (according to the accompanist) to go to the Black Forest, where a postcard from Eckart at the beginning of the scene has asked him to join him.

Baal Abandons the Mother of his Unborn Child.

Scene 7. Flat land, sky, and evening.

This is approximately [12], but without reference to Baal's taking Eckart's women, or having been in prison, and without the two men's wrestling at the end of the scene. It is all shorter, and it appears to come as a surprise to Baal that Sophie is pregnant:

BAAL: Pregnant? That's the last straw. What do you think you're up to? And now I suppose I'll have you hanging round my neck?

ECKART: On principle I don't interfere in your exceedingly shabby human relationships. But at least when a third party is present they should be conducted with some semblance of fairness.

BAAL: Are you going to abandon me on her account? That'd be just like you. She can clear out. She's going downhill. I'm as patient as a lamb. But I can't change my skin.

SOPHIE: You see, Baal, I didn't need to tell you before. It's been slower than I thought, mostly because you didn't like me all that much. I'm in the fourth month.

ECKART: She's showing some vestige of common sense. Once again: I refuse to let my feelings get involved, but I'll wait here till it's all settled.

Sophie then starts begging them to stay, for an hour, for half an hour. She tells Baal: 'Oh yes, it's a beautiful evening, and you like it. But you won't like it when you have to die without another soul there.' 'Yes, I will,' says Baal. And as Sophie shouts that they are degenerate beasts Baal tells Eckart, 'I absolutely insist that you and I leave now.'

In the Years 1907–10 We Find Baal and Eckart Tramping across South Germany.

Scene 8. Countryside. Morning. Wind.

Baal – Eckart

BAAL: The wind's getting up again. It's the only thing you get free in this country, but all it does now is touch my skin. It isn't strong enough for my ears these days. Your fugue hasn't made much progress either.

ECKART: The sounds my fugue is based on are no worse than most. As for the mathematics of it, it's more mathematical than the wind. The landscape keeps getting more mathematical. It's humanity's only prospect. There's already a corrugated iron barn over there; tomorrow there'll be a steel-framed building. The big cities are spreading their standardized limbs across the old landscape. Between all those tall buildings the wind will be measurable.

BAAL: We're the last people to see the flat plain. In forty-nine years the word 'forest' won't be needed. Wood will cease to be used. Mankind will disappear too, if it comes to that. But to stick to our own lifetime, by the time your big cities are built you'll be delirious. Instead of those tall constructions you'll see rats.

ECKART: By then it will take entire typhoons to make you hear the slightest noise.

BAAL: My friend, I want to live without a skin. You're really an evil man. Both of us are. Unfortunately. Here's a poem I've written.

He then reads 'The Drowned Girl', as in [15], after which:

ECKART: You don't seem to have lost much of your power.

BAAL: Everything there is to say about life on this planet could be expressed in a single sentence of average length. That sentence I shall some time or other formulate, certainly before I die.

Scene 9. Countryside.

Night. Baal asleep. Eckart looking at him.

ECKART: This man Baal worries me. He's not light enough any longer. I'm an objective kind of person. It would be simple enough to pick up a piece of chalk and establish the graph of his life on all the house walls. When I think about it, the only thing that keeps me is the fact that his character's if anything getting harder. All the same, I'm the last man to want to witness the enfeeblement that's bound to accompany his decline and death. I'm not a vindictive character. Just lately he's been keeping a very sharp eye on me. It's difficult to tell if he's genuinely asleep now, for instance. There are no fields left for him to graze down. It's starting to rain again; I'd better cover him up.

In the Year 1911 Baal Succumbs to his Predestined Disposition to Murder.

Scene 10. 'Pub.'

Autumn evening. Eckart, Emilie Mäch, and Johann Schmidt in black.

This is essentially [18], with the difference that the waitress is Sophie and that Emilie is present, with a good deal to say. Watzmann is cut, his verse about 'When the hatred and venom' from the 1919 version being now hummed by Emilie. There are no other verses apart from those of the 'Ballad of the Adventurers' sung by Baal.

It starts with Johann asking, 'When's Baal coming?' Then Eckart:

> It's become increasingly clear to me in these last few years that great times are in store for us. The countryside is going to ruin. I've seen photographs of buildings on Manhattan Island which indicate a vast power in the human race. Having reached a high point of insensitivity, mankind is setting to work to create an age of happiness. The years in question will be limited in number; what matters is to be there. For a few weeks I've felt myself becoming increasingly restless.

EMILIE: When's Baal coming?

They discuss who has any money to pay for drinks. Emilie's husband has died. They discuss Baal, before his entrance, somewhat as in [18]. Emilie, who says she has 'come to see the golden boy eight years later . . . You know, I'd feel there was something missing if he didn't somehow or other go completely to pieces,' asks Eckart if he is abandoning him. Eckart says: 'Yes, it's already written on my face. It's obvious to everybody. Only he doesn't realize it yet. Although I keep telling him. As I did today,' then breaks off as Baal arrives.

The first exchanges are much as in [18], but Baal then asks the waitress, 'Is that you, Sophie?' Johann answers:

> Yes, that's her all right. How are you? I'm doing very nicely. It's a very good atmosphere here. Beer.

SOPHIE: Beer.

After Eckart's outburst, where he says he is going back to the forests, Baal says 'Are you off again? I don't believe it, you know. I feel perfectly well myself.' Eckart then tells the story of the man who thought he was well, as told by the Beggar in the Bolleboll–

Gougou scene [13], up to the final 'Did he get well?' (here asked by Baal). 'No.'

Johann(es) makes none of his long melancholy speeches, but when he for the second time says, 'It really is a very good atmosphere here,' he adds, 'Like in the old days.' Emilie thereupon hums her verse, and Baal turns to Eckart:

That girl Johanna Schreiber was with us then.

EMILIE: Oh, the one who killed herself. She's still stuck in a culvert somewhere. They never found her. He's got a wife now, and a nice little coal-merchant's business.

JOHANN: Brandy.

SOPHIE: Brandy.

EMILIE: Have I altered much? I wasn't too bad after you'd finished with me. I don't imagine you're pleased to hear that. For a time I couldn't take any drinks that hadn't been mixed eight times over. My late husband got me off wood-alcohol by hitting me.

BAAL: Nothing doing.

EMILIE: Give me a cigar.

SOPHIE: Cigar.

EMILIE: Give me the strongest schnaps; it's all right. And I'll go to bed with any of you that knows his business. Technique: that's what I'm interested in. What are you looking at now?

She claims to have drunk more than any of them. Baal replies: 'You were never drunk, you had amazing control of yourself, you never were worth anything. That girl back there, for instance, who was very close to me once, is absolutely used up. She was a first-class phenomenon on this planet.' As Emilie weeps, Baal sits by her and makes a formal declaration:

. . . If you for your part still have some inclination towards my body, then I, being unaccustomed ever in my life to let any sort of offer go by, would now like to say this to you: my outward circumstances will make me incline towards you in six years at the most, by which time you will have achieved a total age of forty years.

He smashes the light and sings, and Eckart's murder follows much as in [18].

Baal on the Run. 10 Degrees East of Greenwich.

Scene 11.

Almost identical with [9].

Baal Dies Wretchedly among Woodcutters in the Year 1912.

Scene 12. Night, rain, woodcutters playing cards.

Baal on a dirty bed.

This is considerably cut, but otherwise very close to [21]. The main difference is as the last woodcutter is leaving, after wiping Baal's forehead. Baal calls him closer and says:

. . . I agree. [Ich bin einverstanden.]
MAN: What with?
BAAL: With everything.
MAN: But it's all over now.
BAAL: That was excellent.
MAN: Off we go, then.
BAAL: Hey, give me the book.
MAN: But you haven't any light.

In Baal's final speech there is no 'Dear God' and no 'Dear Baal'. He calls for Eckart, not for his mother, and his last words are 'It's better in the doorway. Man! Trunks. Wind. Leaves. Stars. Hm.'